Emeril's

THERE'S A CHEF IN MY WORLD!

RECIPES THAT TAKE YOU PLACES

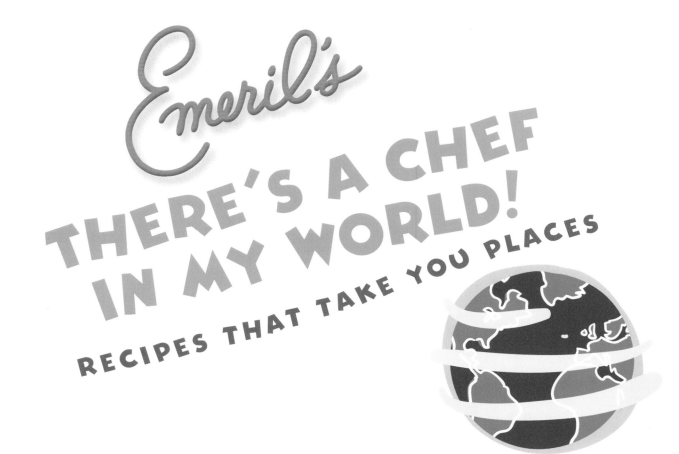

Emeril's
THERE'S A CHEF IN MY WORLD!
RECIPES THAT TAKE YOU PLACES
BY EMERIL LAGASSE

Illustrated by Charles Yuen

Photographs of Emeril Lagasse
and children by Quentin Bacon

HarperCollins*Publishers*

For information on Emeril Lagasse or his books and products, please contact:
Emeril's Homebase
829 St. Charles Avenue
New Orleans, Louisiana 70130
Tel: (800) 980-8474
(504) 558-3940
www.emerils.com

Emeril's There's a Chef in My World!: Recipes That Take You Places

Interior photos of Emeril Lagasse and children by Quentin Bacon

Jacket models: (front, l-r) Daniel Manuel, Sam Manzi, Bryar Lynne Falvey; (back, l-r) Lily Halpern, Robert Zaffiris, Sunshine Sanchez

All illustration, drawings, photography by Quentin Bacon, text, and recipes are the property of Emeril's Food of Love Productions LLC, used by permission.

Thanks to the following for use of additional photographs: Amelia Anderson: pp. 60, 94; Jane Becker: p. 142; Matthew Benjamin: pp. 127, 138; Robin Benjamin: pp. 31, 88, 114, 122, 158; SoRelle Braun: p. 32; Barbara Campisi: pp. 41, 109, 156, 157; Margaret Chadbourne: p. 45; Richard Emmert: p. 167; Julia Gaviria: pp. 116, 118; Ryan Germick: p. 50; Jeph Gurecka: pp. 35, 183; Barbara Hertel: pp. 101, 102; Ted and Betsy Lewin: p. 73; Wendy Lynch: pp. 62, 104; Antonia Markiet: p. 178; Shari Mendelson: p. 160; Rachel Orr: p. 171; Judith Page: pp. 42, 78, 80, 83, 92, 146, 152, 155, 172, 196; Karin Paprocki: p. 38; Martha Rago: pp. 120, 187; Monica Stamm: pp. 180, 192; Lauren Velevis: p. 176; Amy Vinchesi: pp. 68, 87, 128, 141, 184, 194; Charles Yuen: pp. 37, 48, 54, 58, 64, 71, 74, 96, 106, 112, 132, 134, 136, 175, 191

Library of Congress Cataloging-in-Publication Data

Lagasse, Emeril.
Emeril's there's a chef in my world! : recipes that take you places / by Emeril Lagasse ; illustrated by Charles Yuen ; photographs by Quentin Bacon.
p. cm.
ISBN-13: 978-0-06-073926-3 (trade bdg.)
ISBN-10: 0-06-073926-6 (trade bdg.)
1. Cookery, International—Juvenile literature. I. Title: There's a chef in my world!. II. Title.
TX725.A1L224 2006   2005015133
641.59—dc22   CIP
                                                                                    AC

Design by Charles Yuen
❖
First Edition

To Meril Lagasse, our blessed baby girl who
has brought so much joy—
May your life be filled with love and delicious
moments.

To my countless friends who have embarked
upon the mission of good food with me—
May cooking continue to be your passport to
the world.

—ACKNOWLEDGMENTS—

EMERIL'S THERE'S A CHEF IN MY WORLD! is the culmination of a longtime dream of mine to help expand the culinary worlds of children, and I thank the following folks from the bottom of my heart for helping me make this dream come true:

- My family—Miss Hilda and Mr. John, who brought me into this world, my incredible and always supportive wife, Alden, and my wonderful children, Jessie, Jillie, E.J., and Meril, who ARE my world

- Charlotte Martory, my dear friend and a terrific mom who has amazing talent, vision, and dedication to this and any project she touches, not to mention being an amazing cook—I say thank you

- The Emeril's Culinary Team—Chef David McCelvey, Chef Bernard Carmouche, Marcelle Bienvenu, Charlotte Martory, Trevor Wisdom, Alain Joseph, and Laura Martin —whose well-traveled taste buds and test kitchen diligence contributed immeasurably to this project

- Marti Dalton, for her amazing creative energy

- Mara Warner, for keeping my world manageable!

- My compadres and fellow world navigators, Eric Linquest, Tony Cruz, Scott Farber, and Tony Lott

- Jim McGrew, for his expert legal counsel in all matters

- My Homebase family, for being the solid place in my world I always enjoy coming home to

- All the folks in my restaurants who work so hard at reaching out to the world through incredible food: Emeril's Restaurant, NOLA, and Emeril's Delmonico Restaurant in New Orleans; Emeril's New Orleans Fish House and Delmonico Steakhouse in Las Vegas; Emeril's Restaurant Orlando and Emeril's Tchoup Chop in Orlando; Emeril's Restaurant Atlanta; and Emeril's Restaurant Miami

- Photographer Quentin Bacon and his assistant, Amy Sims

- Jim Griffin, my friend and agent, who has expanded my world considerably

- All the folks at HarperCollins Children's Books, who saw this project as a possible way of making the world a smaller place for our universal family:

- Susan Katz, Publisher

- Kate Jackson, Senior V.P., Associate Publisher and Editor-in-Chief

- Antonia Markiet, Senior Executive Editor extraordinaire, whose impeccable vision shapes every project

- Martha Rago, Executive Art Director

- Robin Benjamin, Editor, whose tireless eagle-eyes and devotion to detail are invaluable

- Amelia Anderson, Designer

- Rachel Schoenberg, Designer

- Diane Naughton, V.P. of Marketing

- Carrie Bachman, Director of Publicity (Adult Division)

- Milena Perez, Senior Publicist (Adult Division)

- Katherine Hanzalik, Assistant Publicist (Adult Division)

- Jim McKenzie, Director of Children's Online Marketing

- John Vitale, V.P., Director of Production

- Lucille Schneider, Director of Production

- Mark Rifkin, Managing Editor

- Amy Vinchesi, Senior Production Editor

- And once again to the creative genius of illustrator Charles Yuen, whose illustrations bring his colorful, beautiful vision of the world to each and every page of this book

Thank you all.

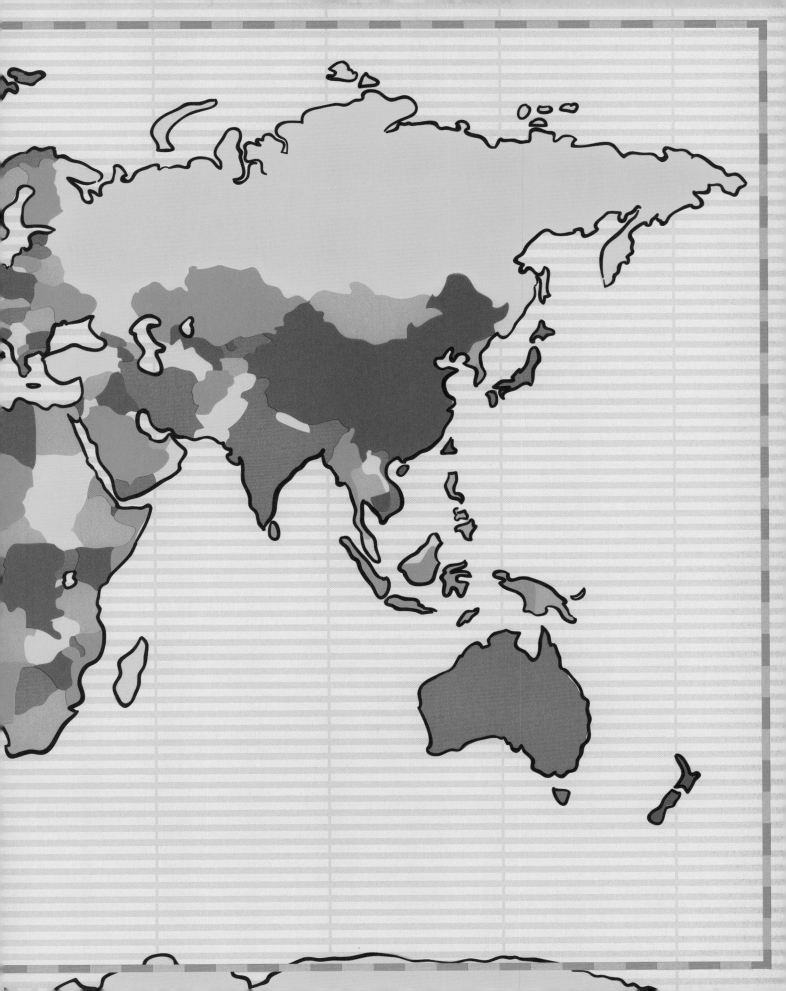

CONTENTS

A GUIDE TO SIDES 131

THE BREAD MAP 149

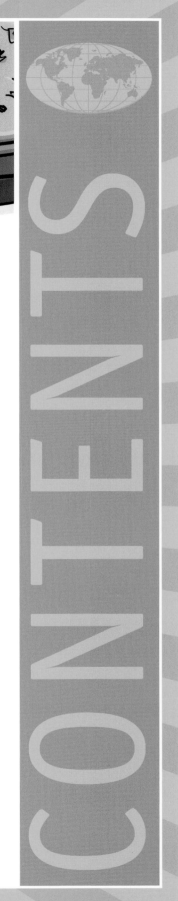

CONTENTS

Emeril's THERE'S A CHEF IN MY WORLD!

RECIPES THAT TAKE YOU PLACES

WELCOME TO MY WORLD!

I'm so happy that you have joined me on this wonderful journey that began a few years back with the publication of my first children's cookbook, EMERIL'S THERE'S A CHEF IN MY SOUP!: *Recipes for the Kid in Everyone.*

When I began writing EMERIL'S THERE'S A CHEF IN MY SOUP!, my goal was to excite young folks about food and cooking so that they might enjoy participating in meals prepared at home with friends and family. As it turned out, not only were we successful in reaching them, but parents too seemed to heed our call to return to enjoying home-cooked meals prepared with love by all members of the family. The natural succession to EMERIL'S THERE'S A CHEF IN MY SOUP! was the publication of a second book that was geared toward families cooking together, EMERIL'S THERE'S A CHEF IN MY FAMILY!: *Recipes to Get Everybody Cooking.* In that book, we really encourage EVERYONE in the family to take a part in the creation and enjoyment of nourishing, wholesome meals. After all, what is more important than spending time with loved ones, and what better way to enjoy time spent together than in the kitchen, cooking and eating! And I can't tell you how happy it has made me to see so many families trying to return to this wonderful way of life, nourishing bodies and spirits alike.

But guess what? I'm here to tell you that folks want more! Friends everywhere have been coming up to me and asking, "What's next?" They want to take it to the next level, so to speak, and to build on the foundation of basics that we've taught them in these previous books.

Well, the answer to this question was easy. I began thinking about how traveling and experiencing other cultures around the world has not only enriched my life and my creativity but has made me feel a part of a larger universal family. Wouldn't it be great, I said to myself, if my next project could broaden the horizons of others and allow them to experience different corners of the world and to feel a part of a bigger family, too? So that leads us to the publication of EMERIL'S THERE'S A CHEF IN MY WORLD!: *Recipes That Take You Places.* In this book, I show you how easy it is to prepare many of your favorite well-known ethnic dishes—and maybe introduce you to a few new ones that you have yet to enjoy. The recipes included here span the globe and take you to some very exciting culinary places. Within many of the recipes there is a little section I call "Did You Know . . ." that contains an interesting tidbit about the recipe, its ingredients, or its origins. Your supermarket will have

most of the ingredients you need to cook the super dishes in this book. Many markets have ethnic specialty sections that offer a variety of ingredients. But if you can't find something in your grocery store, you can check online or in specialty food catalogs. What better way to introduce your family to the different cultures of the world without even leaving your home!

Now, EMERIL'S THERE'S A CHEF IN MY WORLD! also takes you and your families to the next step in terms of recipe difficulty—but don't worry, there is still something here for everyone. Some recipes are very simple, where the youngest members of the family can help by stirring ingredients together. Others either require adult supervision or are for the older children in the family. I have been careful to point out which recipes require additional safety measures using the same caution icons from my previous children's cookbooks (see page 5), so this should take a lot of the guesswork out of choosing which recipes are appropriate for specific members of the family. Since some of these recipes may be new to you, we have also tried to give serving suggestions for dishes so that you might prepare an entire meal from this book, if you like. Many of the dishes from different countries go together quite well because of an overlapping of flavors and seasonings. This is often the result of historical and geographical factors. For example, the cuisine of Northeast Italy has a lot of influence from Austrian cooking. This is because that region was part of the Austro-Hungarian Empire for many years. You may find that this is a great opportunity to explore a little world history and geography and also create your own culinary mixes and matches while you're all cooking together.

So, come on, dig in, read up, and get cooking! Take your family on a trip to Italy, Spain, Sweden, Africa, South America, the Far East, or any number of other places that are represented here, just by cooking and enjoying good food at your dinner table. If your family, like many American families, has lost its connection to its heritage, then this might be a wonderful time to reconnect with the foods that your ancestors enjoyed. Or, if after cooking from EMERIL'S THERE'S A CHEF IN MY WORLD! you find that your family has a particular love for the foods of a certain country, then by all means take this as an opportunity to go out and purchase a more comprehensive cookbook devoted entirely to foods from that country. Your family's horizon will be broadened considerably, and your meals together will become times for learning and exploration. So, in the spirit of a hungry traveler, around the world we go!

Happy Cooking and Eating, as always! Or, as they say in different places around the world—Bon Appétit! Mangia Bene! ¡Buen Provecho! Mag's gut schmecken! Kale orexe! Dobar tek! Mani deuseyo! . . .

Chef Emeril

A GOOD COOK IS A SAFE COOK!

Hey, cooking is a lot of fun! I love everything about working in the kitchen—how the food looks, feels, and smells, and of course how it tastes when you're all done. But it's really important to remember that cooking is serious stuff. If you don't pay attention in the kitchen, you can get hurt very easily—and I want to be sure that doesn't happen. So before we get started, let's go over some ways to be safe in the kitchen.

ASK FOR HELP!

- Remember *always* to ask permission from your mom or dad or any adult in charge before you begin cooking.

- Never cook by yourself. It's always a good idea to have an adult nearby, especially when using sharp knives or graters, electrical appliances, hot burners, and the oven.

- You can do a lot of things yourself if you're careful, but ask for help when you need it—like lifting heavy pots. Being smart in the kitchen is important!

- You have to dress right for the kitchen—not to look good but to be safe and comfortable. Cooking clothes should be roomy but not too loose. Loose clothing can get caught on equipment, and you always have to be especially careful around an open flame. Long sleeves should be rolled up tight so they don't get in the way.

- Loose, long hair is a big no-no! If you have long hair, tie it back so it doesn't get in your way or into the food.

- Most jewelry isn't safe in the kitchen. Don't wear anything that dangles. If you wear a watch, be sure it's waterproof.

BE PREPARED!

- Always review the recipe you will be preparing before you begin. Make sure you have all the ingredients you need, and that all the tools and equipment are ready. Believe it or not, I still do this.

- If you don't understand how to do something, ask an adult to explain it to you before you begin cooking.

- I like to measure out all my ingredients before I start. I cut, chop, mince, and mix ahead when I can, too. It makes cooking a breeze.

To help you stay safe, we've included little safety icons. You and your folks will know with one quick look how careful you'll need to be. Here's what they are and what they mean:

 This recipe requires adult supervision. With the exception of easy sandwiches, which don't require the use of sharp objects, heat, or electrical appliances, this symbol will be on almost all the recipes.

This recipe requires the use of sharp objects such as knives or graters. You need an adult around to help, and you need to pay attention!

 This recipe requires cooking either on the stovetop or in the oven. You have to be very, very careful and have an adult in the kitchen.

This recipe requires handling hot objects from either the stovetop or the oven. Be sure to use oven mitts or pot holders!

 This recipe requires the use of electrical appliances.

 This recipe requires the handling of raw meat, poultry, eggs, or seafood, which can carry germs. Wash your hands and tools with warm to hot water and soap before and after you touch these ingredients!

BE CLEAN!

● Cleanliness is very important in the kitchen. I know I sound like a grown-up but it's really true. You want the food you serve to be healthy and safe.

● Make sure you wash your hands well both before and after handling raw foods such as meat, poultry, eggs, and seafood. These items can sometimes contain harmful germs such as salmonella that can make you very sick. This can be prevented if you wash your hands and any tools that touched raw ingredients (knives, cutting boards, etc.) very well with warm to hot water and soap (preferably antibacterial), both before and after handling such ingredients.

● Here's a big secret we professional chefs have that I'll let you in on: It's a smart idea to clean up as you go along. That way, any tools that you need again will be clean and ready for you, and you'll have plenty of room on your counter to work. Best of all, you won't end up with a mountain of dirty dishes just when you want to be sitting down to enjoy your yummy creation.

- Never put knives or other sharp objects in sinks filled with water and other utensils—you can cut yourself when you reach into the water. It also damages the blades. It's best when working with knives to wash them well with soap and water as soon as you're finished with them.

- Cutting boards should always be washed with soap and warm water after each use. When you're using them to prepare raw meat or poultry, you have to be even more careful than usual! Unclean cutting boards can pass germs along to other foods. When in doubt wash, wash, wash.

STAY COOL WHEN COOKING WITH FIRE!

- It's really important to have an adult close by whenever you're cooking on the stove or in the oven, and they should be around from start to finish, when you turn the appliance off. Don't ever use the stove—or the oven—when you're home alone!

- Be extra careful of hot surfaces when cooking. It's easy to tell when a stovetop with a gas (open) flame is on; it's less obvious on stoves with electric or radiant burners, which are just as hot. Check your stovetop or oven controls carefully before you get to work.

- Pot holders and oven mitts rule in the kitchen! If you're not sure if something is hot, use pot holders or mitts just to be on the safe side. And hey—it's really important that pot holders and oven mitts are dry when you use them. If they're wet, the heat will go right through them and burn you faster than you can say, "Bam!"

- Never, ever leave food unattended while it's cooking!

- Always remember that the outside surface of the oven also gets hot when the oven is on, so don't lean against it when it's on.

- When cooking on top of the stove, always remember to turn your long pot handles to the side or toward the center. But make sure they're not over an open flame. They shouldn't hang over the edge of the stove, either—someone might walk by and knock into them by accident.

- Keep as far away as possible from hot, bubbling liquids. The bubbles can pop and splatter, and that can really burn. It's also a good idea to use long-handled wooden spoons to stir hot things.

- When moving heavy pots filled with hot liquids or when lifting heavy roasting pans out of the oven, you need to be smart. If you're sure you can do it, use pot holders and be really careful. If you think even for a minute that the pot or pan is too heavy for you, don't try to do it yourself. Ask an adult to help you!

Remember always to uncover a hot pot so that the side of the lid farthest away from you tilts up first. This way the steam will be as far away from you as possible. Steam burns can really hurt! The same thing goes for draining a pot that is full of hot liquid—always pour out, away from you, so that the liquid and steam do not burn your hands or your face.

If you do happen to burn or cut yourself, or in case of a fire, call an adult *immediately*!

KNOW YOUR TOOLS AND BE PATIENT!

Kitchen tools are just like any other tools—you have to know how to use them the right way. This is for your safety and also to help you take care of your tools. If you're not familiar with the right way to hold and use knives or other equipment, ask your mom or dad or the supervising adult to show you, or check out our techniques section (pages 14–27) for the right ways to use most kitchen equipment.

When learning how to work in the kitchen, be patient. It's better to practice any technique slowly—particularly chopping, slicing, or mincing. That way you can be precise and safe. You will be surprised to see that with just a little practice, you'll become good at it in no time.

Watch out using graters—they're as sharp as knives! It's real easy to scrape fingers and knuckles when you're not paying attention.

You have to be really careful when using electrical appliances such as the food processor, toaster, microwave oven, toaster oven,

blenders, and mixers. These are powerful tools that should be used with caution. Here are some quick tips to follow at all times:

—Always be sure your hands are dry when you plug or unplug something.

—Never, ever put your hands or fingers inside any electrical appliance when it's on.

—Remember to pull your hair back and not wear dangling jewelry.

—Hey, make sure the lid on your blender is on tight—if it's not, your food will go all over the kitchen.

—Always turn your mixer *off* before scraping down the sides of the bowl or adding ingredients. If a spoon or spatula gets caught in the turning beaters, you'll ruin the mixer and maybe hurt yourself, too.

—When you turn the mixer back on after adding ingredients, start on the slowest speed. That way, your ingredients won't splash all over you.

—Food processors are great tools to use but they require special caution in order to be used safely. The blades are very sharp—be extra careful when removing or washing them. If you need to scrape down the sides of the bowl, do so with a long-handled rubber spatula. Never use your fingers for this! Also, it is especially important to always use the "feed tube" when adding ingredients to a processor that is already turned on. If you need to add something that won't fit through the feed tube, turn the processor off and remove the top. Do not under any circumstances attempt to turn the processor back on until the top is in place and the safety lock is engaged. Most newer food processor models already have safety features to protect you, but it never hurts to be extra careful!

THE NUTS AND BOLTS

HERE ARE SOME of the tools you'll use most often in the kitchen.

1 | KNIVES

chef's knife

bread knife (serrated edge)

paring knife

butter knife

2 | CUTTING BOARDS

wood

plastic

3 | PASTRY CUTTER

4 | MIXING BOWLS

metal

glass

plastic

Note: Plastic or glass bowls should always be used when a recipe calls for a nonreactive bowl. Metal "reacts" with acidic foods such as vinegar and lemon juice, and this makes the food taste funny.

5 SPOONS

wooden   metal   serving   slotted   skimmer

6 COLANDERS

plastic   metal

7 STRAINERS

coarse mesh   fine mesh   sieve   sifter

8 MEASURING CUPS

glass   plastic   metal

9 MEASURING SPOONS

plastic   metal

10 WHISK

11 | SPATULAS AND TURNERS

rubber spatula   metal turner   plastic turner   wood turner

Note: Always use plastic or wood for nonstick pans so you don't damage their surfaces.

12 | TONGS

plastic   metal

13 | LADLE

14 | VEGETABLE PEELER

15 | VEGETABLE BRUSH

16 | GRATERS

box grater   single-sided   microplane

Note: A box grater has four sides: a single long slot for roughly slicing soft items such as cheese; a shredder side with large, widely spaced holes for shredding soft cheese, fruit, or vegetables; a coarse grating side for fruit and veggies and hard cheese; and a fine grating side for hard cheese, nuts, spices such as nutmeg, or for zesting citrus fruits (this will give you a very fine, almost powdery consistency). The single-sided grater usually has only coarse and fine grating capabilities. A microplane is another wonderful tool for zesting and finely grating.

17 | ZESTER

18 | KITCHEN SCISSORS OR SHEARS

19 POTATO MASHERS

20 GARLIC PRESS

21 APPLE CORER

22 PASTRY BRUSH

23 SKEWERS

metal   bamboo

Note: Always soak bamboo skewers in water for 30 minutes before using.

24 INSTANT-READ THERMOMETER

25 BASTERS

bulb   brush

26 SQUEEZE BOTTLE

27 ROLLING PIN

28 KITCHEN TIMER

29 PASTRY BAG WITH TIPS

30 OVEN MITTS AND POT HOLDERS

31 | MIXERS

handheld   standing electric   paddle attachment

32 | BLENDER

33 | FOOD PROCESSOR

34 | JUICERS

35 | WIRE RACK

reamer   stationary

36 | SALAD SPINNER

37 | SALAD TOSSERS

skillet

saucepan

loaf pan

muffin pan

baking sheet

griddle pan

baking dish

Dutch oven

steamer insert

39 | DOUBLE BOILER

40 | RAMEKIN/CUSTARD CUP

41 | COOKING AIDS

paper muffin-tin liners

plastic wrap

parchment paper

aluminum foil

GOOD THINGS TO KNOW

LET'S GET STARTED

WASHING

Fresh veggies and fruits should always be rinsed well under cold running water and then patted dry with paper towels before using. Berries and dried beans should be rinsed well and then "picked over," which simply means picking out and discarding any bad or blemished pieces. Some veggies, such as potatoes, need to be scrubbed well with a vegetable brush. Mushrooms need to be brushed with a soft-bristled brush in order to remove any loose dirt and, if washed, should not be allowed to soak in water. Meat, poultry, and seafood should be washed before using, too. Simply rinse under cold water and then pat dry with paper towels before continuing.

CLEANING LEEKS

Leeks must be carefully washed to remove the sandy soil that often hides between the leaves. First you must trim the root end from the leek. Then cut away any of the tough upper portion of the leek that you will not be using. Cut the leek in half lengthwise. Rinse the leek thoroughly under cool running water, making sure to allow the water to run between the leaves to remove any sand or soil. Dry thoroughly before proceeding.

PEELING

Some fruits and veggies peel easily with a vegetable peeler. Place the food (such as a carrot, cucumber, potato, apple, or pear) on a cutting board and hold firmly with one hand. Using the other hand, scrape the peeler down the length of the food. Keep turning as you go, so that you remove all of the peel.

Other foods, such as onions and garlic, are peeled differently. Use a sharp knife to cut a little off of both ends. Then use your fingers to peel away the dry, tough outer layers. For garlic, press down on it with the palm of your hand to loosen the skin. It will then peel off very easily.

CHOPPING

When chopping round foods like potatoes or carrots, the first thing you should do is cut off a small piece from one side so that it doesn't roll away while you're cutting it. Place this flat part down on the cutting board. Then, hold one side of the food firmly with one hand and cut the food to the shape or size desired. The more you chop, the smaller the pieces will get.

CUBED **ROUGHLY CHOPPED** **FINELY CHOPPED** **MINCED**

When it comes to chopping, onions are in a league all their own! Once they're peeled, cut them in half lengthwise and place them flat side down on the cutting board. Then, while holding the root end with your fingers, make many lengthwise cuts all the way down to the cutting board. Then turn your knife and cut across the lengthwise cuts. Pieces of onion will fall away on the cutting board. The closer your cuts are to one another, the smaller the pieces of onion will be!

Mincing garlic is easy! Separate the head of garlic into cloves. Peel as described on page 14, then use your chef's knife or a paring knife to cut the cloves lengthwise and then crosswise into small pieces. (Another way to do this is with a garlic press, which is really easy and safe—and fun! Just put the garlic into the press, close it, and press real hard. Little pieces of garlic—just the right size—will come out of the holes!)

Fresh herbs can be chopped, too. Remove the leaves from any tough, woody stalks and chop with a chef's knife. Chives are easily chopped this way, or can be "snipped" using kitchen shears. Simply hold the bunch of chives in one hand and cut into small pieces with the scissors held in your other hand.

GRATING

When grating hard foods, like carrots or potatoes, hold the grater with one hand and the piece of food firmly in the other. Rub the end of the veggie downward over the holes, back and forth over a large mixing bowl or piece of waxed paper, and the grated pieces will fall through the holes. Be very careful not to grate your fingers— that hurts! Soft foods, such as cheese, are really easy to grate!

CORING APPLES

- **With an apple corer:** Hold the apple firmly on your cutting board. Center the apple corer over the core and press down firmly until you feel the corer hit the cutting board. Twist and pull corer out of the apple, and the core should come right out.

- **With a paring knife:** Cut the apple in half. Cut each half in half again. Place the apple on the cutting board and cut the core away from the apple.

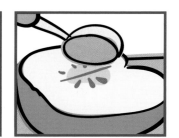

- **With a melon baller:** This is the easiest way to core an apple! Cut an apple in half. Place the apple half on the cutting board, core side up. Hold the melon baller in your other hand and center it over the core of the apple. Press down into the apple and twist. A round piece of apple core should come right out.

HULLING STRAWBERRIES

Place the strawberry on the cutting board and hold the pointed side with one hand. Using a paring knife, cut across the top to remove the stem.

FRUITS WITH PITS (SUCH AS PEACHES, NECTARINES, CHERRIES, PLUMS)

To remove the pit, simply cut the fruit in half along the indentation, then twist the two halves apart.

PEELING MANGOES

Mangoes have a large, flat, oblong seed that extends almost the entire length of the fruit, making them tricky to peel. I find that the best way to peel a mango is to hold the fruit firmly against the cutting board and cut along each side of the pit to remove two large sections. Each section can

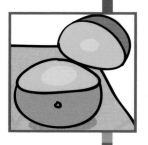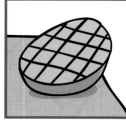

then be cubed in a crosshatch pattern: Make crosswise cuts through the flesh, just to the skin. Press up on the skin side of the section and the cubes will stand out. You may then cut the cubes away from the peel with a knife.

ZESTING

You can "zest" any citrus fruit (oranges, lemons, limes, or grapefruits). Using a "zester," it's really easy. Simply pull the zester down the side of a piece of

fruit, pressing at the same time so that the zester removes tiny strips of the outermost layer of peel. If you don't have a zester, a fine grater or microplane works too. Over a bowl or a piece of waxed paper, rub the side of the fruit along the grater while lightly pressing down. The small pieces of zest will fall through the grater. Sometimes a recipe calls for a larger strip of zest—then simply run a vegetable peeler across the skin of the fruit to remove a portion of the outermost, colored layer of skin. Be sure you get only the colored part of the peel: The white part is bitter!

JUICING ORANGES, LEMONS, LIMES, OR GRAPEFRUIT

Citrus fruits may be juiced in several ways. The easiest way is to cut the fruit in half crosswise, and then, while holding the fruit halves over a bowl to catch the juice, use your hands to squeeze the juice from the fruit. If you own a "reamer," simply hold one fruit half in one hand and insert the reamer into the fruit with the other hand while turning and pushing the reamer to extract the juice. Some folks have stationary juicers that are really a combination of a reamer and a shallow bowl or plate. These are easy to use—simply press the cut side of an orange, lemon, lime, or grapefruit down onto the cone-shaped reamer portion of the dish and twist with a continual downward pushing motion. The bowl portion of the juicer will collect the juice as you turn the fruit. Of course, if you have an electric juicer you can use that as well, but please be sure to follow the manufacturer's safety instructions and watch those fingers!

REMOVING CORN FROM THE COB

Hold the ear of corn in one hand and rest it on the thicker end so that it is standing up on the cutting board. Have an adult use a large chef's knife and, starting at the tip and with a downward motion, cut the kernels from the cob. Turn the cob with every cut so that you get all the kernels. To get even more goodness, you can also scrape the corncobs with the back side of the chef's knife or with a spoon—this will release some of the milk from the corn. Add any juices to the cut kernels. Discard the cobs.

TRIMMING MEAT

It's a good idea to trim the excess fat off of meat before cooking. Simply use a very sharp knife and follow the line between the meat and the fat. If a little fat is left, that's okay.

PEELING AND DEVEINING SHRIMP

Shrimp should be deheaded, peeled, and deveined before using them for most recipes in this book. If you've never done this before, don't worry—it's easy! Hold the tail of one shrimp between the thumb and forefinger of one hand while grasping the head with the thumb and forefinger of the other hand. Pinch lightly where the head

attaches to the tail while pulling it away from the tail, and the head should come right off. The thin outer shell, or peel, is easily removed by grasping one section at a time near where the legs are attached and peeling in a circular motion up and over the tail of the shrimp. The entire peel will usually come off in two or three motions. Once the peel is gone, run the tip of a sharp paring knife down the upper length of the tail of the shrimp, where you will sometimes see a dark vein. Remove the vein with your fingers or by running the shrimp under cold water. If a recipe instructs you to "butterfly" shrimp, that simply means making a deeper cut down the back of the shrimp so that the flesh opens up to resemble a butterfly.

CRACKING AND SEPARATING EGGS

To crack an egg, hold it firmly in one hand while you hit the middle part (not too hard!) against the rim of a bowl. Then take both hands and grasp the cracked edges and pull apart. It's always a good idea to crack an egg into a separate bowl before adding it to a recipe so that you can see if any bits of shell fell into the egg. (If so, remove them before adding the egg to the recipe!) Sometimes a recipe will call for just egg yolks or egg whites. To separate eggs and use either the yolk or white only, crack the egg lightly and pull the halves apart, carefully letting the white drip into a cup. Keep the yolk in the eggshell. Gently move the yolk from one eggshell half to the other, letting the white drip into the cup until only the yolk is left in the shell. Be careful not to break the yolk so that it bleeds into the egg white.

CUTTING DOUGH WITH COOKIE CUTTERS

When cutting shapes out of rolled-out dough with cookie cutters, make sure to press down firmly to get a clean cut. And hey—if you don't happen to own any cookie cutters, don't worry! You can also use the rim of a sturdy glass or bowl. Measure the diameter of what you want to use to make sure it's the correct size, and then place the glass or bowl upside down onto the dough and press firmly, just as you would with a cookie cutter. Depending on the rim, this can make a clean cut. If not, use the tip of a sharp knife and trace the outer edge of the glass or bowl. Remove the glass or bowl and repeat to form the remaining cuts.

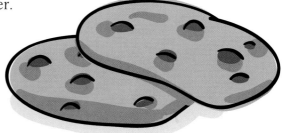

CUTTING CHICKENS

If a recipe calls for a whole chicken cut into pieces, please don't try to cut one up yourself. This is really hard and very dangerous. Either have your parents do it for you or buy a cut-up chicken at the grocery store.

REMOVING SAUSAGE FROM CASING

Sometimes sausage comes stuffed in "casing," which keeps it together. To remove the sausage from the casing, use the point of a sharp knife to cut the tip off of one end of the sausage link and squeeze from the bottom up to force the meat mixture out.

HOW TO KNOW WHEN ENOUGH IS ENOUGH

MEASURING

It's best to use individual ¼-, ⅓-, ½-, and 1-cup measuring cups when you can—it's the easiest and most accurate way to measure things. When measuring dry ingredients such as flour, sugar, or rice, use a metal or plastic measuring cup like that shown at right. Dip the appropriate-size measuring cup into the ingredient that is to be measured, then use the flat side of a knife or your hand to level off the top.

When measuring liquids, use glass or plastic measuring cups that you can see through. Fill until the liquid comes to the appropriate line on the cup, checking at eye level to make sure you've measured the correct amount.

Measuring spoons are easy to use. For dry foods, just dip the spoons into whatever you're measuring, then level off the top. For liquids, such as oil or vanilla extract, hold the spoon in one hand and pour with the other. Make sure to hold the spoon level, and always fill it all the way to the top!

DETERMINING CONTAINER CAPACITY

If you're not sure of the size of a saucepan, baking dish, or other container, simply use a measuring cup to fill it with water. Count the number of cups it takes to fill the container and then figure out its size by referring to the equivalents chart on page 27.

NOW WE'RE COOKING

MIXING

Just another term for combining things, usually with a "mixer," which has beaters instead of spoons. Lock the beaters into the mixer, lower the beaters into the mixing bowl, then turn the power on slowly. As the mixture becomes more blended, you can increase the speed.

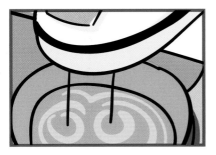

BEATING

This means mixing things together quickly so that air is added to the mixture and it becomes smooth and creamy. It's usually done with a mixer, but you can also beat things with a spoon—it just takes a little elbow grease!

STIRRING

Use a spoon to stir in a circular motion until the ingredients are all blended.

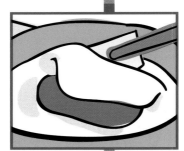

FOLDING

This is a way of mixing things together very gently so that they stay fluffy. Use a large plastic or rubber spatula and, instead of stirring, place it into the bowl and combine the ingredients with two or three up-and-over, or "folding," motions. Don't overmix!

SIFTING

This is done to make sure there are no lumps in dry foods like flour or sugar. Just hold the sifter over a bowl and shake from side to side (some sifters have knobs to turn or handles to squeeze).

CREAMING

This refers to beating butter and sugar together very well until it becomes light and "creamy."

SOFT OR STIFF PEAKS

These terms are used when beating things like heavy cream or egg whites. After you turn the mixer off and lift the beaters out of the bowl, if a little of the mixture comes up where the beaters were, forming soft mounds that stay up, those are soft peaks. When recipe calls for stiff peaks, beat a little longer until the mixture stands straight up and does not tip over when lifting out the beaters. Do not overbeat or the mixture will separate.

SCRAPING DOWN BOWL

This is done to make sure everything gets mixed evenly. Just hold the edge of the mixing bowl in one hand, then run a plastic or rubber spatula all the way around the inside of the bowl to "scrape down" the sides.

EGGS

Eggs come in different sizes. When using eggs for the recipes in this book, always use the ones labeled LARGE.

WORKING BUTTER INTO FLOUR

You can do this with a pastry cutter, two forks or butter knives, or your fingers. The main thing is that the butter is rubbed into the flour so that only small pieces of butter are visible and the rest has been combined with the flour. When it's done, it will look like small crumbs.

SOFTENING BUTTER

If a recipe calls for butter to be softened, it means at room temperature—not straight from the refrigerator. If you forget to take the butter out to soften, try placing it in a microwave-proof bowl and microwave on high for 5 to 10 seconds. This works great.

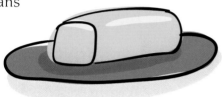

CLARIFYING BUTTER

Clarified butter refers to butter in which the liquid and milk solids have been removed, leaving only pure butterfat. This is needed for certain recipes in which the milk solids or the watery component of butter would interfere with proper recipe results. It's easy to do: Simply heat butter over low heat in a small saucepan until it is completely melted and bubbles a bit. The milk solids will rise to the top and will form a bubbly, white layer. This should be skimmed off the top with a small spoon and discarded. The second layer is the pure yellow butterfat—spoon this into a bowl for saving, making sure not to disturb the very bottom layer, which is a cloudy, white, watery substance that should be discarded.

KNEADING DOUGH

Place the dough on a lightly floured surface. Use one hand to firmly press into one side of the dough. Pick up the other side of the dough with your other hand and fold it over, again pressing into the dough. Pick up the opposite edge of the dough and do the same. Repeat this process for as long as instructed in the individual recipe directions. The dough should become smooth and elastic. If the dough gets sticky, sprinkle with a bit more flour. You can also knead dough in an electric mixer if your mixer has a dough hook. Check manufacturer's instructions.

ROLLING DOUGH

Place the dough on a lightly floured surface and sprinkle the top with flour. Using a rolling pin, roll while pressing down on the dough. Begin by rolling front to back, then switch directions and roll side to side. If the rolling pin sticks, sprinkle a little more flour. Continue rolling until the dough is the desired size and thickness.

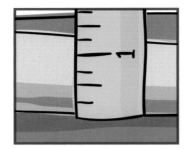

MEASURING THICKNESS OF DOUGH

Until you have a lot of practice with this, it's a good idea to keep a ruler handy. This is an easy way to see if you've rolled your dough out to the correct thickness.

ROLLING AND TRIMMING DOUGH FOR PIES

For pies, dough is usually rolled out to a thickness of $1/8$ inch. The easiest way to transfer this thin dough to the pie pan is to roll the dough directly onto the rolling pin once you have reached the desired thickness. Position the rolling pin over the pie pan and carefully unroll the dough, easing it into the pie pan as you go. Once the dough is fitted into the bottom and corners of the pie pan, use kitchen scissors to trim a smooth, even edge that extends $1\frac{1}{2}$ to 2 inches beyond the edge of the pie pan. For a single-crust pie, fold the cut edge under and tuck inside the pie pan. You may then press or crimp the edges of the dough to form a decorative border—this may be done with either your fingers or a fork. For a double-crust pie, leave the edges of the bottom crust hanging after trimming and lightly brush the edges with either eggwash or water to moisten slightly. Fill the shell with the filling. Roll out the second portion of dough that will be the top crust of the pie as instructed above. Transfer it to the rolling pin as before and position the dough over the top of the filled pie. Carefully lay the dough over the top of

Single Crust

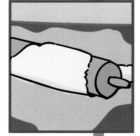

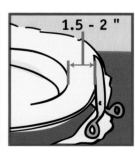

Double Crust

the pie and cut the edges so that they are even with the edges of the bottom crust. Press lightly to seal the edges, then fold the edges under as before. Again, press or crimp the edges to form a decorative border. Double-crust pies often have slits cut into the top crust to allow steam to escape—this may be done with the tip of a paring knife.

WORKING WITH PHYLLO DOUGH

When preparing a recipe using frozen phyllo dough, it is important to allow the frozen phyllo to thaw in the refrigerator for at least 1 day and up to 2 days. If the phyllo is thawed on the kitchen counter, it will develop wet spots that will cause the sheets to stick together.

Once the phyllo has thawed in the refrigerator and you are ready to prepare the recipe, transfer the phyllo to the kitchen counter for an hour or so to allow it to come to room temperature. Remove the phyllo from the box and remove any plastic wrapping. Carefully unroll the sheets and place them on a clean, dry area of your work space. Cover the phyllo stack with a sheet of plastic wrap, then top this with a clean, damp kitchen towel. This is very important, as the paper-thin sheets of phyllo dry out very quickly if not covered in this manner. Remove 1 sheet of phyllo at a time from the stack and, using a pastry brush, lightly coat the entire surface with either melted butter or oil, as the recipe instructs. (Make sure to re-cover the phyllo stack while you are working with the removed sheet.) Repeat with additional sheets, as the recipe instructs. It is important to brush each sheet thoroughly. If instructed to cut the phyllo in any manner, use a very sharp knife for a clean cut.

Any unused sheets of phyllo should not be refrozen. However, if properly wrapped in plastic wrap and refrigerated, they may be used in other recipes for several days.

USING A PASTRY BAG

When a recipe calls for the use of a pastry bag, follow these tips for surefire success: Insert the metal or plastic tip into the pastry bag and press downward so that it fits securely in the bottom of the bag. While holding the bag in one hand, use your other hand to fold the top, open end of the bag down over the hand holding the bag. Using a spoon or spatula, transfer the substance that is to be piped into the bottom of the bag. Do not fill the bag too high or it will be difficult to use. Unfold the top of the bag and close the bag in your hand. Twist the bag once or twice so that the mixture is forced to the bottom. Pipe by holding the bag firmly in your palm and squeezing from the top. Use the fingers of your opposite hand to guide the bag as you work. Tip: If you do not have a pastry bag, most of the time it is easy to substitute a plastic food storage bag. Simply cut one of the bottom corners off the bag so that an opening is left that is the approximate size of the pastry tip you have been instructed to use. Proceed as directed for using a pastry bag.

BASTING

Basting is when you brush, spoon, or drizzle liquid—such as butter, meat drippings, or stock—over food as it cooks. Doing so helps to keep foods moist, adds flavor and color, and also helps form a crisp outer layer, especially for things like roast turkey or baked bread. You can baste by using a small brush, by spooning the liquid over cooking food with a large spoon, or by drizzling the liquid with the help of a bulb baster. If you don't have a brush made especially for basting, any small brush such as a pastry brush will work just fine.

BLANCHING

Blanching is done when foods such as vegetables and fruits are plunged into boiling water briefly, then quickly removed and usually transferred to cold water to stop the cooking process. This lightly cooks items that don't need lengthy cooking, and on such foods as tomatoes and peaches it can be used to loosen the skins so that they may be peeled easily.

GREASING A PAN

Greasing helps keep baked goods from sticking to the pan. It's easy to do this with your hands, but if you don't want to get your hands "dirty" then try using a paper towel to spread the shortening, oil, or butter. Just make sure you don't miss any spots!

Pans and other utensils also can be "greased" by spraying them with nonstick cooking spray. Simply shake the can well, hold it 6 to 12 inches away from the item, and spray until the item appears to be coated with a thin film of grease.

PROOFING YEAST

This is a way of making sure the yeast is working! Let it sit for about 5 minutes in a warm liquid. If it's working, you will see lots of foam and little bubbles rise to the surface.

SAUTÉING

This method of cooking comes from the French word meaning "to jump." It's a very accurate description because when you sauté, you quickly fry food in a small amount of fat. It tends to make the food pop and crisp quickly, so be sure to stir the mixture often and to keep an eye on it.

MELTING CHOCOLATE IN A DOUBLE BOILER

Fill the bottom part of a double boiler with about 2 inches of water. Insert the top part of the double boiler and place the chocolate in it. Set on the stovetop and simmer on low heat, stirring occasionally until the chocolate is melted. If you don't have a double boiler, you can use a medium saucepan for the bottom part and a metal bowl large enough to sit on top of the saucepan without touching the water in the bottom.

TOASTING THINGS

Many recipes call for toasted things, such as nuts or coconut and sometimes bread crumbs or croutons. This is pretty easy to do—just make sure you keep a close eye on whatever you're toasting because some foods toast quicker than others! You'll need either a toaster oven for small amounts or an oven for larger amounts, as well as a baking sheet large enough to hold whatever you're toasting in one even layer.

Make sure the oven rack is in the center position and preheat the oven to 350°F. Spread the desired amount of sweetened flaked coconut or nuts of choice on a baking sheet and make sure they are spread evenly in one single layer. Whole nuts are best for toasting, though halves are okay, too. If the pieces are too small, this timing will be wrong and the nuts can easily burn. You can also chop after toasting if needed. Bake in the oven until just golden and very fragrant, 5 minutes for coconut and 8 to 10 minutes for most nuts. Using oven mitts or pot holders, carefully remove the baking sheet from the oven and transfer to a wire rack to cool. Use as desired or store in an airtight container, preferably in a cool location. Nuts will keep for up to 2 weeks after toasting. Coconut usually gets less crispy after a day or two.

IS IT DONE YET?

TESTING THE HEAT OF A PAN
You can test the heat of a pan by dropping a teaspoon of water in it. The pan is hot enough to cook in when the water "dances" into drops across the bottom.

TESTING WITH TOOTHPICKS
This is an easy trick! Insert a toothpick into the center of a cake near the end of the cooking time—if it comes out clean when you pull it out, the cake is done. If you can see gooey stuff or bits of crumbs sticking to it, then it needs a bit more cooking time.

THERMOMETER USAGE
Some recipes in this book suggest using an instant-read thermometer when things need to be at a certain temperature. Though this is not always necessary, a thermometer does help you make sure that things are cooked enough. Thermometers also help when cooking with yeast, because you usually need to add warm water or other liquid to it in

order for it to start working. A thermometer will tell you if the liquid is too hot or too cold. (If you use a thermometer, make sure that it is inserted far enough into whatever you're testing so that you get a true temperature.)

FORK-TENDER

When you insert a fork into something and it goes in easily, then it is said to be fork-tender.

MEAT DONENESS

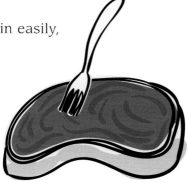

Because some meat may contain germs that can make you sick, it's a good idea to cook your meat until it's no longer pink inside. This is called being "cooked through." Even better, if you have an instant-read thermometer, simply insert the tip into the meat (there is usually a mark on the thermometer that shows how far it should be inserted), wait a few seconds until the temperature stops rising, and then read the number. For beef, medium well to well done is 150° to 165°F. For chicken, turkey, or pork, always cook to at least 160°F.

When testing for doneness on meat such as roast chicken and turkey, it is important that you place the thermometer in the deepest part of the joint between the leg and thigh, and equally important that the tip of the thermometer is not touching a bone. Have an adult help you master this technique!

COOKING WITH EGGS

When a recipe instructs you to cook eggs until they are "set," this means that the egg mixture should no longer be liquid or runny and should be firm when moved slightly.

KICK UP THE FLAVOR!

DRIED VS. FRESH HERBS

Most of the recipes in this book call for dried herbs, since this is what most folks have at home. It's really easy to kick them up a notch by rubbing them between your fingers before adding them to the recipe. They will release more flavor this way! And hey, if your mom or dad has an herb garden and you have access to fresh herbs, feel free to use them in recipes. Just take the leaves off of the stems and chop into small pieces with a knife. Remember, though, that if you want to use fresh herbs, you'll have to use about 3 times the dry amount called for in the recipe to get the same amount of flavor.

PEPPER

When a recipe calls for ground black pepper, the kind you buy in spice jars or tins is just fine. However, if you have a pepper mill at home, there's nothing like the flavor of fresh-ground pepper.

White pepper is a less pungent form of pepper that has a slightly different, milder flavor. It is most often used in light-colored dishes or those made with mild-flavored foods. If you don't have white pepper at home, simply substitute an equal amount of black pepper.

SALT

Kosher salt is an additive-free, coarse-grained salt. Some cooks prefer kosher salt's unique texture and flavor for specific uses. If you cannot find kosher salt in your grocery store, you can substitute sea salt or regular table salt. If you choose to substitute table salt, use only about half the amount called for.

BABY BAM

YIELD: About ¾ cup

INGREDIENTS

3 tablespoons paprika

2 tablespoons salt

2 tablespoons dried parsley

2 teaspoons onion powder

2 teaspoons garlic powder

1 teaspoon ground black pepper

1 teaspoon dried oregano

1 teaspoon dried basil

1 teaspoon dried thyme

½ teaspoon celery salt

TOOLS

Measuring spoons • small mixing bowl • wooden spoon • airtight container

DIRECTIONS

Here's something to season your food the way adults do with Emeril's Original Essence. Give food another dimension by sprinkling Baby Bam into everything, from soups and sauces to pizza and hamburger patties. You fearless bammers out there can kick this up a notch by adding cayenne (I'd start with about ¼ teaspoon, and then take it from there). Place all the ingredients in a small mixing bowl and stir well to combine, using a wooden spoon. Then store in an airtight container for up to 3 months.

MEASUREMENT EQUIVALENTS

3 teaspoons = 1 tablespoon

4 tablespoons = ¼ cup

1 cup = ½ pint = 8 ounces

2 cups = 1 pint = 16 ounces

2 pints = 1 quart = 32 ounces

4 quarts = 1 gallon = 128 ounces

1 stick butter = 8 tablespoons = ¼ pound = ½ cup

CHAPTER 1

TOAD IN THE HOLE

Here's a traditional English breakfast that comes from Yorkshire, a county in the northern part of England. These popovers have chunks of flavorful smoked sausage baked in a super-simple batter. The batter puffs up and gets crispy on the outside yet remains light and airy on the inside—oh, baby! Nobody knows exactly how this dish got its name, but one thing's for sure: The "toad" is the sausage!

INGREDIENTS

1 scant cup all-purpose flour (about 15 tablespoons)

2 teaspoons dry mustard

½ teaspoon salt

1½ teaspoons Emeril's Original Essence or Baby Bam (page 27) or other Creole seasoning

1 large egg

1¼ cups whole milk

2 tablespoons bacon drippings or vegetable oil

6 ounces smoked sausage, cut crosswise into ½-inch pieces

½ cup chopped yellow onion

TOOLS

Measuring cups and spoons • cutting board • chef's knife • sifter • medium mixing bowl • whisk • nonstick muffin tin • oven mitts or pot holders

DIRECTIONS   CAUTION

1. Position rack in lower third of oven and preheat the oven to 425°F.

2. Sift the flour, mustard, and salt into a medium mixing bowl and add the Essence or other Creole seasoning.

3. Make a well in the center of the flour mixture and add the egg and ¼ cup of the milk. Using a whisk, mix the egg and milk into the flour mixture a little at a time, adding the remaining cup of milk little by little to form a smooth batter. Do not overmix. Set the batter aside to rest for at least 30 minutes.

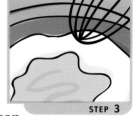

STEP 3

4. Grease the wells of a nonstick muffin tin with ½ teaspoon each of the bacon drippings or vegetable oil. Divide the sausage and onion evenly among the wells. Bake for 12 to 14 minutes, until the onion is lightly golden, the sausage is golden around the edges, and the drippings or oil are bubbling. Using oven mitts or pot holders, remove the muffin tin from the oven and divide the batter evenly among the wells, about 3 tablespoons of batter for each well. Using oven mitts or pot holders, carefully return the muffin tin to the oven and cook for 18 to 20 minutes, until popovers are puffed and golden brown on top. Using oven mitts or pot holders, remove the popovers from the oven and serve immediately, as they will deflate if you let them sit after baking.

STEP 4

HINT

For an easy breakfast, make the batter the night before, cover, and refrigerate. Preparing the recipe will be a breeze the next morning. And hey—these make great afternoon snacks, too!

TORRIJAS (torr-EE-hass)

This is the Spanish take on French toast and is especially enjoyed during Easter Holy Week in Spain. This dish is served with confectioners' sugar and cinnamon, but you can kick yours up a notch with a drizzle of your favorite breakfast syrup! In France, this same dish is called Pain Perdu, and in England it is known as Eggy Bread. Almost every culture has its own version of this yummy dish!

DID YOU KNOW . . .

Pain Perdu means "lost bread" in French. It's such a popular dish all over the world because it's a tasty and thrifty way to use stale bread that you would have to throw away otherwise.

INGREDIENTS

3 large eggs

3 tablespoons granulated sugar

2 teaspoons ground cinnamon

$^3/_4$ teaspoon vanilla extract

Pinch of freshly grated nutmeg

Pinch of salt

$1^3/_4$ cups whole milk

$^1/_4$ cup heavy cream

8 ($^1/_2$-inch thick) slices day-old French or other crusty peasant-style bread, or slice fresh bread and leave the slices out for an hour or two to harden slightly

2 tablespoons vegetable oil

2 tablespoons unsalted butter

2 tablespoons confectioners' sugar

Syrup (optional)

TOOLS

Measuring cups and spoons • cutting board • bread knife • large mixing bowl • whisk • large nonstick skillet • tongs or fork • metal spatula • plate • aluminum foil • small mixing bowl • oven mitts or pot holders

DIRECTIONS   CAUTION

1. In a large mixing bowl, combine the eggs, granulated sugar, 1 teaspoon of the cinnamon, vanilla, nutmeg, and salt, and whisk to dissolve the sugar. Add the milk and cream and whisk to combine.

2. Place 4 slices of the bread in the bowl with the batter and let sit until well moistened, 30 seconds to 1 minute.

3. In a large nonstick skillet, heat half of the oil and melt half of the butter over medium heat.

4. Carefully transfer the 4 soaked bread slices to the hot pan and cook until golden brown, about 3 minutes per side, turning once. Transfer to a warm plate and cover with aluminum foil to keep warm. Repeat with the remaining ingredients.

5. In a small mixing bowl, combine the remaining teaspoon of cinnamon with the confectioners' sugar.

6. To serve, divide the Torrijas among 2 to 4 plates. Dust with the cinnamon-sugar and serve with syrup, if desired.

LATKES
(LAHT-kuhs)

These Eastern European treats can best be described as fried potato pancakes—and once you've had one, you will see why they are legendary worldwide! Traditionally served at Hanukkah, latkes make wonderful treats for any time of the year and any time of the day or night—for breakfast, as after-school snacks, or as hors d'oeuvres before dinner. Try them as suggested here, with applesauce and sour cream—the most traditional way to serve them.

DID YOU KNOW . . .

Hanukkah, the Festival of Lights, commemorates the miracle that happened during the re-dedication of the Hebrew Temple in Israel in 165 B.C. A one-day supply of oil was supposed to have burned for eight days. Today the miracle is celebrated by lighting candles on a special candleholder called a menorah for eight days. The oil that these potato pancakes are fried in is supposed to symbolize the burning oil from the miracle.

34

INGREDIENTS

2½ pounds baking potatoes, peeled

1 medium yellow onion, grated

2 large eggs, lightly beaten

2 tablespoons all-purpose flour

1 teaspoon salt

¼ teaspoon ground white pepper

¼ teaspoon baking powder

1 to 1¼ cups vegetable oil, for frying

1 cup applesauce

1 cup sour cream

TOOLS

Measuring cups and spoons • vegetable peeler • box grater • fork or whisk • colander • clean kitchen towel or cheesecloth • medium mixing bowl • wooden spoon • large skillet • spoon • metal spatula or tongs • paper towel–lined baking sheet • oven mitts or pot holders

DIRECTIONS   CAUTION

1. Preheat the oven to 200°F.

2. Using a box grater, coarsely grate the potatoes. Watch your fingers!

STEP 2

3. Place the potatoes in a colander lined with a clean kitchen towel or cheesecloth and let the potatoes sit for at least 15 minutes to release some of their liquid. Pick up the four corners of the towel or cloth and bring them together, then tightly wring the towel in the sink so that any extra liquid is squeezed from the potatoes.

4. Transfer the potatoes to a medium mixing bowl and add the grated onion, beaten eggs, flour, salt, pepper, and baking powder. Using a wooden spoon, stir until thoroughly combined.

5. In a large skillet over medium-high heat, add ¼ cup of the oil to the pan. When the oil is hot, spoon the potato mixture, 2 tablespoons at a time, into the skillet to form individual cakes. You should be able to fit 4 or 5 latkes in the pan at a time. Using the back of a spoon, flatten each latke so that it resembles a pancake. Cook until golden brown, about 2 to 3 minutes. Using a metal spatula or tongs, carefully flip the latkes over, making sure to watch out for any splattering oil. Cook the latkes until the second side is golden brown, about 2 minutes longer.

STEP 5

6. Remove the latkes from the pan and set aside to drain on a paper towel–lined baking sheet. You can keep them warm in the heated oven while you cook the remaining latkes. Add more oil as needed and continue to fry the latkes in batches, making sure not to overcrowd the pan.

7. To serve, place a dollop of applesauce and/or sour cream in the center of each latke. Serve warm.

HUEVOS RANCHEROS

(WAY-vohs rahn-CHEH-rohs)

This is a hearty breakfast dish from Mexico and means "rancher's eggs." I like to use fried eggs, but you can use sunny-side-up or whatever kind of eggs you like. If you have any ranchero salsa left over, you can serve it another time with chips or quesadillas. Just cover the salsa and put it in the refrigerator and it will keep for 1 week.

DID YOU KNOW . . .

Mexican cowboys are called "vaqueros." Ranchers need extra-hearty breakfasts because they work so long and hard.

DIRECTIONS

CAUTION

1. Heat 1 tablespoon of the oil in a small saucepan over medium-high heat. Add the onion and sauté for 3 minutes, stirring occasionally to keep from sticking. Add the garlic and cook, stirring for 30 seconds. Stir in the tomatoes, lime juice, jalapeño, cilantro, salt, and pepper. This is called a salsa. Bring the mixture to a boil and then reduce the heat to low. Simmer the salsa, uncovered, over low heat for 10 minutes. Remove from the heat and set aside. Cover with the lid to keep warm.

CAUTION

Always handle jalapeño peppers with rubber gloves and be careful not to touch your eyes or skin.

INGREDIENTS

Salsa:

2 tablespoons vegetable oil

1/3 cup chopped yellow onion (about 1/2 small onion)

1 teaspoon minced garlic (about 1 medium clove)

2 1/2 cups chopped tomatoes (about 2 medium tomatoes)

1 tablespoon fresh lime juice

1 tablespoon seeded, minced jalapeño (about 1/2 small jalapeño)

2 tablespoons chopped fresh cilantro

1/2 teaspoon salt

1/4 teaspoon ground black pepper

Eggs:

1 cup diced chorizo sausage (about 5 ounces)

6 corn tortillas

6 large eggs

3/4 teaspoon salt

3/4 cup grated queso fresco or Monterey Jack cheese

TOOLS

Measuring cups and spoons • cutting board • chef's knife • juicer (optional) • rubber gloves • box grater • small saucepan with lid • 2 large nonstick skillets • wooden spoon or heat-resistant spatula • slotted spoon • paper towels • 3 large plates • dry cloth (optional) • aluminum foil • oven mitts or pot holders

2. Heat a large nonstick skillet over medium-low heat. Add the chorizo and cook, stirring, 8 to 10 minutes, until the sausage is golden brown and cooked through. (Be careful when stirring so that the grease from the chorizo doesn't pop out of the pan.) Remove the chorizo with a slotted spoon and drain on a paper towel–lined plate. Set aside. Reserve 1 1/2 tablespoons of the drippings from the sausage.

3. Heat a clean nonstick skillet over medium-low heat. Add 1/2 teaspoon of oil to the pan and place one tortilla in the oil. Cook for 1 minute and turn. Cook an additional 30 seconds. The tortilla will be slightly golden but still soft. Transfer the warm tortilla to a plate and cover with foil to keep warm. Continue to cook the remaining tortillas, using about 1/2 teaspoon of oil for each tortilla.

4. In the same skillet, heat half of the reserved drippings from the chorizo over medium-high heat. One at a time, carefully break 3 eggs into the skillet, making sure that the edges of the eggs don't touch one another. Season the eggs with 1/8 teaspoon salt each, and fry each egg about 1 minute. Using a spatula, carefully flip the eggs and fry for 1 minute longer, or to the desired degree of doneness. Transfer the eggs to a plate and sprinkle each egg with 2 tablespoons of the grated cheese.

5. Using the remaining chorizo drippings, cook the remaining 3 eggs and sprinkle with 2 tablespoons of cheese each.

6. To serve, place 1 tortilla on each plate. Top each tortilla with a fried egg and cheese. Sprinkle chorizo over the egg and top with salsa. Serve warm.

STEP 6

GERMAN APPLE PANCAKE

This super-huge pancake is fit for a king! It's made from a simple batter that is poured over the sautéed apples and then baked for a puffy treat you eat hot from the oven. It is traditionally eaten with confectioners' sugar, but kick yours up with maple syrup, if you like! The Germans call this "appelpfannkuchen." I call it great!

INGREDIENTS

4 large eggs, lightly beaten

1 cup whole milk

1 cup all-purpose flour

$\frac{1}{2}$ teaspoon vanilla extract

3 tablespoons unsalted butter

2 large apples, peeled, cored, and thinly sliced (page 15)

$\frac{1}{2}$ teaspoon ground cinnamon

$\frac{1}{8}$ teaspoon ground nutmeg

Pinch of salt

$\frac{1}{3}$ cup packed light brown sugar

Confectioners' sugar

Maple syrup (optional)

TOOLS

Measuring cups and spoons • cutting board • paring knife • vegetable peeler • apple corer • large mixing bowl • whisk • heavy ovenproof 12-inch skillet (preferably nonstick) • wooden spoon • oven mitts or pot holders • sifter

DIRECTIONS CAUTION

1. In a large mixing bowl, combine the beaten eggs, milk, flour, and vanilla, and whisk until just blended, being careful to not overmix. Set the batter aside to rest at least 20 minutes.

2. Position rack in center of oven and preheat the oven to 450°F.

3. In a heavy ovenproof 12-inch skillet, melt 2 tablespoons of the butter over high heat. Add the apples, cinnamon, nutmeg, and salt and cook, stirring frequently, until the apples are soft and lightly golden around the edges, about 6 minutes.

4. Add the brown sugar and cook, stirring, until the apples are caramelized and very soft, 2 to 3 minutes longer. Add the remaining tablespoon of butter and stir to melt.

5. Working very quickly, pour the batter evenly over the top of the apples. Using oven mitts or pot holders, transfer the skillet to the oven and bake until the pancake is golden brown and puffed, about 15 minutes. Don't be alarmed when you see the edges of the pancake puff up over the top of the pan—this is supposed to happen!

STEP 5

6. Using oven mitts or pot holders, remove the skillet from the oven and serve the pancake immediately, sprinkled with sifted confectioners' sugar or drizzled with maple syrup, as desired.

MANGO LASSI

(LAH-see)

The lassi is a popular Indian chilled yogurt drink. It's very refreshing, especially because the weather and the food in India can be pretty hot!

I like it for breakfast because it's a yummy and nutritious way to start the day. Feel free to substitute or add other fruits, as you like. Strawberries and/or blueberries would be wonderful additions, as would peaches . . . any ripe, soft fruit that you love!

DiD YOU KNOW . . .

Mangoes are native to southern Asia and were brought to the Western Hemisphere in the seventeen and eighteen hundreds. Now they're grown wherever the climate is frost free, like Californa, Hawaii, and the Caribbean Islands, to name a few places.

INGREDIENTS

2 mangoes, peeled and cut into chunks ($2\frac{1}{2}$ to 3 cups cubed mango) (page 16)

$\frac{1}{2}$ cup fresh orange juice

$\frac{1}{2}$ cup ice cubes

2 tablespoons honey

$1\frac{1}{4}$ teaspoons rose water

$1\frac{1}{2}$ cups plain yogurt

TOOLS

Measuring cups and spoons • cutting board • paring knife • juicer (optional) • blender

DIRECTIONS

CAUTION

In a blender, combine all of the ingredients and process on high speed until very smooth and frothy, about 2 minutes. Serve immediately.

41

STRAWBERRY-FILLED SCONES

Scones are really popular around the world. In England, Scotland, Ireland, the Netherlands, and Germany, they are often enjoyed during afternoon tea time. But in America we like scones for breakfast. Scones also make great lunchbox treats and after-school snacks, or try taking them on a picnic. If you don't care for strawberry jam, use your favorite flavor in the recipe instead.

INGREDIENTS

2¼ cups all-purpose flour, plus more for shaping the scones

2 tablespoons plus 2 teaspoons sugar

1 tablespoon baking powder

1 teaspoon salt

½ cup (1 stick) unsalted butter, cold and cut into small pieces

¾ cup plus 2 tablespoons buttermilk

¼ cup strawberry jam

2 tablespoons whole milk

TOOLS

Measuring cups and spoons • baking sheet • parchment paper • large mixing bowl • sifter • rubber spatula (optional) • spoon • rolling pin • 2 metal spatulas • pastry cutter or chef's knife • pastry brush • oven mitts or pot holders

DIRECTIONS   CAUTION

1. Position rack in center of oven and preheat the oven to 400°F. Line a baking sheet with parchment paper and set aside.

DID YOU KNOW . . .

In Ireland, folks believe that you have to prick the dough with a fork or make a small cut with a knife before baking scones to let the fairies out!

2. In a large mixing bowl, sift the flour, 2 tablespoons of the sugar, baking powder, and salt.

3. Add the butter to the dry ingredients and cut into the flour, using your hands or a pastry cutter, until the butter is the size of small peas.

4. Add the buttermilk and mix, using your hands or a rubber spatula, just until the liquid is incorporated, being careful not to overmix.

5. Divide the dough in half, and lightly sprinkle your work surface with flour. Place half of the dough on the floured surface and roll out into an 8-inch disk about ½ inch thick. Spread the jam over the top of the disk, being sure to leave an inch of space all along the outer edge of the dough.

STEP 5

6. On the work surface, lightly flour the second half of the dough and roll it out into a disk the same size as the first. Carefully, using two floured metal spatulas, pick up the dough and lay the second disk on top of the first. Use your fingers to pinch the edges of the dough together so that they are sealed.

STEP 6

7. Using the pastry cutter, or a chef's knife dusted with flour, cut the dough into 6 triangles. Separate the triangles and lay them on the parchment-lined baking sheet, about 2 inches apart. Using a pastry brush, brush the tops of the scones with the milk, sprinkle with the remaining 2 teaspoons of sugar, and place in the oven.

8. Bake the scones until the tops are golden brown, about 25 minutes. Using oven mitts or pot holders, remove the scones from the oven and serve immediately.

STEP 7

SWISS MUESLI

(MYOOS-lee)

This granola-like cereal was invented by a Swiss doctor and makes a wonderful, healthy breakfast. You can eat it plain or spooned over yogurt or fresh fruit and drizzled with extra honey if you like! This recipe makes a big batch, so it can double as a great lunch box or after-school snack. Any leftovers can be stored in an airtight container at room temperature for up to 2 weeks.

INGREDIENTS

3 cups old-fashioned rolled oats

1 cup slivered (not sliced) almonds

1 cup coarsely chopped walnuts

½ cup honey

½ cup coarsely chopped dried apples

½ cup coarsely chopped dried apricots

TOOLS

Measuring cups • cutting board • chef's knife • large baking sheet • oven mitts or pot holders • wooden spoon • large mixing bowl • large rubber spatula

DIRECTIONS   CAUTION 👁 🔪 🔥 🧤

HINT

It is important that you use slivered, not sliced, almonds for this recipe. Sliced almonds are thinner and will burn during the baking time required.

1. Position rack in center of oven and preheat the oven to 300°F.

2. On a large baking sheet, combine the oats, almonds, and walnuts, and bake for 30 minutes, stirring once after 15 minutes. Be careful here! (To do this, remove the baking sheet from the oven using oven mitts or pot holders and mix the hot cereal with a wooden spoon, and then return to the oven.)

STEP 2

3. Using oven mitts or pot holders, remove the baking sheet from the oven and transfer the cereal to a large mixing bowl. Add the honey and, using a large rubber spatula, stir to combine thoroughly. Add the apples and apricots and stir well. Cool, stirring occasionally. Serve at room temperature.

SIGHTSEEING SNACKS, SALADS, AND STARTERS

CHAPTER 2

SHRIMP AND VEGGIE SUMMER ROLLS

This Vietnamese specialty is a cousin of a Chinese favorite, the egg roll, except it isn't fried. Don't let these rolls intimidate you! The secret is to have all the ingredients set out and ready, assembly line style, so they're easier to put together. If you leave out the shrimp, these make a great vegetarian snack, too. You can also serve them with the Peanut Sauce on page 53.

DIRECTIONS   CAUTION

1. Pour 2 cups hot water into a large mixing bowl and add the cellophane noodles. Soak the noodles until softened, about 20 to 30 minutes. Drain the excess water from the noodles and pat dry with paper towels. Cover and set aside.

2. In a medium saucepan, combine 4 cups water, the ginger, lemon halves, soy sauce, sugar, bay leaves, green onion, garlic, salt, black pepper, and cayenne. Bring the mixture to a boil over high heat.

3. Carefully add the shrimp to the boiling soy sauce mixture and boil for 2 minutes. Remove the pan from the heat and allow the shrimp to stand in the hot mixture for 2 more minutes, until cooked through.

4. Using a slotted spoon, remove the shrimp from the cooking liquid and place in a small mixing bowl. When the shrimp are cool enough to handle, slice in half lengthwise. Using a fine-mesh strainer, strain and reserve $1/2$ cup of the shrimp cooking liquid for the Asian Dipping Sauce.

STEP 4

5. Fill a shallow dish (about 9 inches wide or larger) with warm water. Make sure it's not too hot or the rice paper will tear easily. Place a clean, dry kitchen towel next to the dish. Submerge 1 rice paper wrapper in the warm water and soak it until it is softened, about 30 seconds. Carefully remove the rice paper wrapper from the water and lay it flat on the towel. (Don't worry about drying the top of the rice paper; the excess water will help it to stick together better.)

STEP 5

INGREDIENTS

1 (3¾-ounce) package cellophane noodles

4 cups water

1 (2-inch) piece of ginger, peeled and thinly sliced

1 lemon, halved

¼ cup soy sauce

¼ cup sugar

4 bay leaves

1 tablespoon chopped green onion (green and white part)

1 teaspoon chopped garlic (about 2 small cloves)

1 teaspoon salt

1 teaspoon freshly ground black pepper

½ teaspoon cayenne

20 large shrimp, peeled and deveined (page 17)

10 (8½-inch) round rice paper wrappers

40 small fresh mint leaves

40 small fresh cilantro leaves

3 romaine lettuce leaves, rinsed, patted dry, ribs removed, and torn into bite-size pieces

1 large carrot, peeled and shredded

1 recipe Asian Dipping Sauce

TOOLS

Measuring cups and spoons • cutting board • chef's knife • paring knife • box grater • vegetable peeler • large mixing bowl • paper towels • medium saucepan • slotted spoon • small mixing bowl • fine-mesh strainer • 9-inch shallow dish • clean, dry kitchen towel • large plate • oven mitts or pot holders • damp towels (optional)

6. Place ⅓ cup of the soaked cellophane noodles on the rice paper, about 1 inch from the bottom. Leave about 1 inch on each side, too. Arrange 4 mint leaves and 4 cilantro leaves over the noodles. Layer 4 shrimp halves on top of the herbs. Place 3 to 4 bite-size pieces of lettuce over the shrimp, and pile about 2 tablespoons of shredded carrots on top.

STEP 6

7. Pull the bottom inch of the rice paper over the filling and roll halfway up the rice paper. (Make sure that you wrap tightly, but be gentle so the wrapper doesn't tear.) Fold the sides over the filling and continue to roll up like an egg roll. Place the summer roll, seam side down, on a large plate and cover with a damp paper towel. Repeat the process with the remaining rice paper wrappers and filling.

8. Serve immediately with the dipping sauce, or refrigerate, covered with damp towels, for up to 1 hour before serving.

DID YOU KNOW . . .

Vietnam is part of the Indochinese Peninsula in Southeast Asia, with the South China Sea along its entire west coast. Shrimp and other seafood play a big role in Vietnamese cooking.

ASIAN DIPPING SAUCE

INGREDIENTS

½ cup reserved shrimp cooking liquid from Shrimp and Veggie Summer Rolls

1 tablespoon toasted sesame oil

2 tablespoons rice wine vinegar

2 teaspoons fish sauce

1 tablespoon soy sauce

1 tablespoon sugar

1 teaspoon minced garlic

1 tablespoon chopped fresh ginger

¼ cup sliced green onions (cut on the diagonal)

TOOLS

Measuring cups and spoons • cutting board • chef's knife • vegetable peeler • small mixing bowl • whisk

DIRECTIONS   CAUTION 👁 🔪

1. Combine all the ingredients in a small mixing bowl and whisk until well blended.

2. Set aside until needed and stir well before serving.

TIP

The sauce can be covered and refrigerated in a nonreactive container for up to 3 days.

EDAMAME

(eh-dah-MAH-meh)

These delicious Japanese soybeans are very healthy and a treat that folks around the world go crazy over. They're fun to eat, too—scrape the pod between your teeth to release the flavorful beans inside, or pinch the pod between two fingers and watch the beans pop right out. These are a great afternoon snack, or make a bowl for your family to share before dinner. You're sure to make everyone happy, happy!

DID YOU KNOW . . .

Edamame can be traced as far back as 200 B.C. in Chinese history. They were later introduced into Japanese culture, along with soy sauce, tea, and chopsticks.

INGREDIENTS	TOOLS	
1 pound frozen soybeans	Measuring spoons • steamer • large pot • tongs • large mixing bowl • wooden spoons • oven mitts or pot holders	
1 teaspoon sesame oil		
1 teaspoon kosher salt		

DIRECTIONS

CAUTION

1. Place the soybeans in the top of a steamer set over a large pot of simmering water. Steam until tender, about 5 minutes.

2. Using tongs, transfer to a large mixing bowl and toss with the sesame oil and kosher salt. Serve warm.

CHICKEN SATAY (sah-TAY) WITH PEANUT SAUCE

In India, Thailand, and Indonesia, satay are often made with different types of meat, or even shrimp. But I really like these chicken ones. It's important that you soak the bamboo skewers in water before spearing the chicken. This helps to keep the skewers from burning when they're in the oven. I like to serve Chicken Satay at parties as appetizers because you don't need a fork to eat them.
Just pick up a stick and enjoy!

DIRECTIONS   CAUTION   👁 🔪 🔥 🧤 🖐

1. In a medium mixing bowl, combine the soy sauce, peanut oil, sesame oil, fish sauce, ginger, garlic, coriander, and crushed red pepper. Stir to combine.

2. Using kitchen scissors or a chef's knife, cut the chicken crosswise into thin strips, about 3 inches long by $1/2$ inch thick. Add the chicken strips to the soy mixture and cover tightly with plastic wrap. Wash your hands thoroughly. Place the bowl into the refrigerator and marinate for 2 hours.

3. Position rack in middle of oven and adjust oven settings to broil. Line a baking sheet with heavy-duty aluminum foil and lightly grease the foil.

4. Remove the chicken from the marinade and thread one strip of chicken on a soaked wooden bamboo skewer. Place the satay on the baking sheet. Continue with the remaining chicken and skewers.

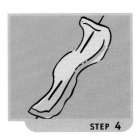

STEP 4

5. Using oven mitts or pot holders, place the baking sheet in the oven and broil for 5 to 6 minutes, until the chicken is cooked through and slightly golden.

CAUTION **Please have an adult help you to use your broiler.**

INGREDIENTS

2 tablespoons soy sauce

1 tablespoon peanut oil

1 teaspoon toasted sesame oil

1 tablespoon fish sauce

1 teaspoon minced fresh ginger

1 teaspoon minced garlic

$1/2$ teaspoon ground coriander

$1/4$ teaspoon crushed red pepper

1 pound boneless, skinless chicken breasts

16 to 18 (12-inch) bamboo skewers, soaked in warm water for 15 to 30 minutes

1 recipe Peanut Sauce

Cilantro sprigs for garnish (optional)

TOOLS

Measuring spoons • cutting board • kitchen scissors or chef's knife • medium mixing bowl • plastic wrap • baking sheet • heavy-duty aluminum foil • oven mitts or pot holders

6. Using oven mitts or pot holders, carefully remove the Chicken Satay from the oven.

7. Serve the Chicken Satay warm, with Peanut Sauce and cilantro sprigs, if desired.

PEANUT SAUCE

This sauce can be made ahead of time, covered, and stored in the refrigerator for up to 2 days.

INGREDIENTS

$1/4$ cup chopped green onions

$2 1/2$ tablespoons chopped fresh cilantro

1 jalapeño, stemmed, seeded, and chopped

1 teaspoon minced garlic

$1/2$ teaspoon minced fresh ginger

$3/4$ cup smooth peanut butter

1 tablespoon toasted sesame oil

$2 1/2$ tablespoons fish sauce

4 teaspoons fresh lime juice (about $1/2$ small lime)

$1 1/4$ cups coconut milk

2 tablespoons hoisin sauce

2 tablespoons honey

TOOLS

Measuring cups and spoons • cutting board • chef's knife • juicer (optional) • can opener (optional) • rubber gloves • food processor • rubber spatula • dipping bowl (for serving)

DIRECTIONS   CAUTION

1. In a food processor, combine the green onions, cilantro, jalapeño, garlic, and ginger. Process on high speed for 30 seconds, stopping to scrape down the sides of the bowl as needed.

> **CAUTION** Always handle jalapeño peppers with rubber gloves and don't touch your eyes or skin!

2. Add the peanut butter and sesame oil and process for 30 seconds, stopping to scrape down the sides of the bowl as needed.

3. Add the fish sauce and lime juice and process to blend, 30 seconds more.

4. Add the coconut milk, hoisin sauce, and honey, processing until smooth and scraping down the sides as needed.

5. Transfer the sauce to a dipping bowl and serve at room temperature with Chicken Satay.

DID YOU KNOW . . .

Satay are a popular street food all over Asia. Almost every country in the world has sidewalk carts with treats to buy as you're walking along.

SPANAKOPITA

(span-uh-KOH-pih-tuh)

These little triangle-shaped pies originated in Greece and are fun and easy to eat. Since this recipe makes a lot, you can reheat them later for an after-school snack. You can even freeze the little pies and reheat them another time.

DID YOU KNOW . . .

Greek foods are often served lukewarm or at room temperature because in Greece it was once believed that serving hot food was unhealthy.

INGREDIENTS

2 (10-ounce) packages frozen chopped spinach, thawed

$1/4$ teaspoon salt

$1/8$ teaspoon freshly ground black pepper

1 teaspoon dried oregano

1 teaspoon dried parsley

1 teaspoon dried basil

1 large egg, lightly beaten

2 tablespoons extra-virgin olive oil

1 tablespoon fresh lemon juice

1 (8-ounce) package feta cheese, crumbled

24 sheets frozen phyllo pastry, thawed (page 23)

$1 1/2$ cups melted unsalted butter

TOOLS

Measuring cups and spoons • juicer (optional) • baking sheet • parchment paper • colander or wire-mesh strainer • medium mixing bowl • wooden spoon • plastic wrap or damp cloth or paper towels • large cutting board • pastry brush • paring knife • oven mitts or pot holders

DIRECTIONS   CAUTION

1. Position rack in center of oven and preheat the oven to 350°F. Line a large baking sheet with parchment paper.

2. Place the spinach in a wire-mesh strainer or colander, place over a sink and drain well. Use your hands or a paper towel to squeeze the excess water out of the spinach.

3. Place the spinach in a medium mixing bowl. Add the salt, pepper, oregano, parsley, and basil. Stir in the beaten egg, olive oil, and lemon juice. Add the feta cheese and mix well to combine. Set aside.

4. Gently unfold the phyllo dough. (Note: It's important to keep a piece of plastic wrap and a damp cloth or paper towel over the phyllo sheets that you are not working with to keep them from drying out. See page 23 on working with phyllo dough.) Lay 1 sheet of phyllo on a large cutting board and gently brush with the melted butter.

5. Place a second phyllo sheet on top of the first and brush with butter. Repeat two more times until you have a stack of 4 phyllo sheets with butter brushed between the layers.

6. Using a paring knife, cut the phyllo sheets lengthwise into 3 strips. Place 2 tablespoons of the spinach filling 1 inch from the bottom end of each strip.

STEP 6

7. Take the bottom right corner of the strip between your thumb and finger and fold over the spinach filling to the left to make a triangle. Gently pull up the bottom left corner and fold up to make a second triangle. Continue folding until you reach the top. Place the triangle, seam side down, on the prepared baking sheet. Brush the completed triangle lightly with butter.

STEP 7

8. Repeat with the remaining strips and phyllo sheets until all of the filling is used.

9. Arrange the triangles 2 inches apart on the baking sheet. Bake for 15 minutes, until golden and heated all the way through. Using oven mitts or pot holders, remove the spanakopita from the oven and cool slightly on the baking sheet.

10. Serve warm or at room temperature.

PORK EMPANADAS

(em-pah-NAH-dahs)

Empanadas are favorites throughout Latin countries. My version here combines a savory meat filling that takes its flavors from Central America, all wrapped up in a simple cream cheese pastry dough that can be made with an electric mixer in no time. If you like, you can substitute thinly rolled refrigerator biscuit dough if you don't have the time to make your own pastry dough.

DID YOU KNOW . . .

Empanadas come from the Spanish word "empanar," which means "to cover in bread." These stuffed pastries are favorites at festivals and are a popular street food, too.

TIP

If you don't have the time to prepare your own dough for this recipe, you can substitute two 4.5-ounce cans of buttermilk biscuits. Simply roll out each biscuit to a 5-inch round about 1/8 inch thick, add the filling, seal, crimp, and bake as described below. The cooking time may vary slightly.

DIRECTIONS

CAUTION

1. Make the pastry: In the bowl of an electric mixer, beat together the cream cheese and the butter until smooth. Gradually add the flour and 1/4 teaspoon of the salt and continue beating until they are thoroughly incorporated.

   CAUTION: Be careful to keep utensils and fingers away from the rotating beaters of the mixer when adding ingredients.

2. Remove the dough from the mixing bowl and transfer to a lightly floured work surface. Knead the dough lightly by hand, then shape dough into a disk and wrap in plastic. Refrigerate the dough for at least 3 hours and up to overnight.

3. While the dough is chilling, prepare the filling: In a medium nonstick skillet over high heat, combine the ground pork, cinnamon, cumin, the remaining salt, allspice, oregano, and crushed red pepper, and cook, using a spoon to

INGREDIENTS

1 (8-ounce) package cream cheese, softened to room temperature

6 tablespoons unsalted butter, softened

1¼ cups all-purpose flour

¾ teaspoon salt

¾ pound ground pork

1¼ teaspoons ground cinnamon

¾ teaspoon ground cumin

¼ teaspoon ground allspice

¼ teaspoon dried oregano leaves

¼ teaspoon crushed red pepper

½ cup chopped yellow onion

1 tablespoon minced garlic

3 tablespoons tomato paste

2 tablespoons cider vinegar

2 tablespoons light brown sugar

¼ cup currants

1 tablespoon capers, drained

4 teaspoons chopped green olives

1 cup water

1 large egg, lightly beaten

TOOLS

Measuring cups and spoons • electric mixer • large mixing bowl • plastic wrap • cutting board • chef's knife • medium nonstick skillet • wooden spoon • rolling pin • small bowl or saucer • pastry brush • fork • paring knife • large baking sheet • nonstick cooking spray • oven mitts or pot holders • cooling rack

break up any clumps, until the meat is golden brown and cooked through, about 6 minutes. Add the onion and cook until soft, about 4 minutes. Add the garlic and cook for 1 minute, stirring constantly. Add the tomato paste, vinegar, brown sugar, currants, capers, and olives, and stir to thoroughly combine. Stir in the water and reduce the heat to medium. Continue to cook, stirring occasionally, until the sauce is very thick and the flavors have come together, about 15 minutes. Remove from the heat and allow to cool completely before proceeding.

> **CAUTION** Please follow the directions for cooking pork on page 26 very carefully.

4. Position rack in center of oven and preheat the oven to 350°F.

5. Place the dough on a lightly floured work surface and sprinkle with flour. Using a floured rolling pin, roll out the dough to a circle about ⅛ inch thick. Using a small bowl or saucer as a guide, cut as many 5-inch rounds of the dough as you can. Set the rounds aside while you gather up the scraps. Press the scraps together and knead lightly to reform the dough into a disk. Roll out as before to a thickness of ⅛ inch and again cut as many rounds as you can. You should be able to get twelve 5-inch rounds of dough.

6. Using a pastry brush, remove any excess flour from the dough rounds.

7. Using a tablespoon measure, top one side of each dough round with about 2 tablespoons of the cooled meat filling. Using a pastry brush, brush the edges of one side of each round with some of the beaten egg, then fold the edges over so that the dough meets to form a half-circle–shaped pie. Using the tines of a fork, press the edges of the dough circle firmly to crimp.

STEP 7

8. Spray a large baking sheet with nonstick cooking spray and place the meat pies on the prepared baking sheet. Using the tip of a paring knife, cut several small slits into the top of each empanada to allow air to escape while baking.

9. Transfer the baking sheet to the oven and bake for 14 to 16 minutes, or until golden brown.

STEP 7

10. Using oven mitts or pot holders, remove the empanadas from the oven and transfer to a cooling rack. Serve warm.

HERBED MEDITERRANEAN YOGURT CHEESE SPREAD

 I just love this appetizer! Yogurt is very popular in Mediterranean countries. Dress yours up by using garlic or chili-infused olive oil. Or, a squeeze of fresh lemon juice will give the cheese a tangy flavor. Use any fresh herbs you like best, such as basil or dill. In addition to the suggestions below, I serve this alongside fresh veggies like carrot sticks, radishes, and celery. For the creamiest results, use whole-milk yogurt instead of the low-fat versions.

DID YOU KNOW . . .

Yogurt goes back some eight thousand years, to the dawn of civilization, and is believed to have been discovered by the Bedouins of the Arabian Peninsula.

INGREDIENTS

2 cups plain yogurt

1 teaspoon kosher or other coarse-grain salt

Freshly ground black pepper

1/2 teaspoon chopped fresh thyme

1/2 teaspoon chopped fresh oregano

1 teaspoon chopped fresh parsley

1 to 2 tablespoons extra-virgin olive oil

Pita wedges, carrot sticks, radishes, celery sticks, cucumber slices, and Kalamata olives, for garnish (optional)

TOOLS

Measuring cups and spoons • cutting board • chef's knife • colander or wire-mesh strainer • medium mixing bowl • cheesecloth • plastic wrap • serving plate

DIRECTIONS   CAUTION

1. Place a colander or wire-mesh strainer over a medium mixing bowl. (Make sure that there is enough room between the bottom of the colander or strainer and the bowl for about an inch of liquid to drain off the yogurt.) Fold a large piece of cheesecloth in half and place inside the colander, draping the edges over the sides.

2. Pour the yogurt into the cheesecloth, and cover the entire bowl with plastic wrap. Place the yogurt in the refrigerator and chill overnight. (The longer the yogurt sits in the colander, the thicker the cheese will be!)

3. Remove the yogurt from the cheesecloth and place on a serving plate. Season with salt and freshly ground black pepper. Sprinkle the thyme, oregano, and parsley over the top of the cheese and drizzle with olive oil.

4. Serve the yogurt cheese with pita bread wedges, veggies, and Kalamata olives. The yogurt cheese will keep, covered, in the refrigerator for 3 to 4 days.

CAPRESE SALAD

(kah-PRAY-seh)

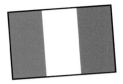

This super-simple, classic Italian salad pairs three of Italy's favorite ingredients: ripe tomatoes, fresh mozzarella cheese, and sweet basil. It was created at the Trattoria da Vincenzo on the island of Capri, in the Bay of Naples, and is favored as a light lunch. Try this refreshing salad at your next summertime cookout!

INGREDIENTS

1 pound vine-ripened tomatoes

½ pound fresh mozzarella cheese

⅓ cup packed fresh basil leaves, plus extra for garnish

¼ cup extra-virgin olive oil

¼ cup balsamic vinegar

1 teaspoon sugar

Salt

Freshly ground black pepper

TOOLS

Measuring cup and spoons • cutting board • serrated knife • chef's knife • large plate or platter • blender • small mixing bowl • whisk

DIRECTIONS   CAUTION

1. Using a serrated knife, slice the tomatoes horizontally about ½ inch thick. Discard the very tops and the bottoms.

2. Using a sharp knife, slice the mozzarella into ¼-inch slices.

3. On a large plate or platter, arrange the tomato and cheese slices in an alternating shingle pattern.

STEP 3

4. Place the basil leaves in a blender with the olive oil and puree until smooth, about 15 seconds.

5. Drizzle the basil oil evenly over the tomatoes and mozzarella. In a small mixing bowl, combine the balsamic vinegar and the sugar and whisk to combine. When the sugar is completely dissolved, pour the vinegar mixture over the tomatoes and mozzarella.

6. Garnish the plate with fresh basil leaves and sprinkle with salt and black pepper to taste. Serve immediately.

SWEDISH CUCUMBER SALAD

This cool and delicious salad combines cucumbers in a quick pickling marinade and is the perfect accompaniment to the Swedish Meatballs on page 104. As a matter of fact, in Sweden, you hardly ever see meatballs served without some version of a cucumber salad along with boiled new potatoes and lingonberries! Try this salad next time you barbecue for a taste of summer. It goes with just about anything that comes off the grill!

DID YOU KNOW . . .

Scandinavian folks love just about anything pickled. Pickling is popular because it is one way of preserving the fresh food of summer through the long, cold winters of Sweden, Denmark, Norway, Finland, and other northern countries.

INGREDIENTS

3 large seedless cucumbers, about 1 pound each, or 4 pounds regular cucumbers

1½ teaspoons salt

⅓ cup white vinegar

2 tablespoons cider vinegar

½ cup sugar

1 tablespoon chopped fresh dill

TOOLS

Measuring cups and spoons • vegetable peeler • small spoon or melon baller • paring knife • cutting board • chef's knife • colander • 2 medium nonreactive bowls • spoon

DIRECTIONS   CAUTION

1. Peel the cucumbers and cut in half lengthwise. Using a small spoon or a melon baller, scoop out the seeds and watery center from each half, forming a shallow groove down the center.

2. Using a sharp paring knife, slice the cucumbers crosswise as thinly as possible, ideally about ⅛ inch thick.

STEP 2

3. Place the cucumbers in a colander and sprinkle with the salt. Using clean hands, toss to combine the cucumbers with the salt and allow to stand, refrigerated, for at least 1 hour and up to 2 hours.

4. Using clean hands, squeeze handfuls of cucumber slices to release any excess liquid and transfer to a medium nonreactive bowl.

5. In another medium nonreactive bowl, combine the white vinegar, cider vinegar, and sugar, and stir until the sugar is completely dissolved. Pour the vinegar mixture over the cucumbers and add the chopped fresh dill. Stir to thoroughly combine and serve, or refrigerate up to 12 hours or overnight and serve cold.

SESAME PEANUT NOODLE SALAD

This Chinese side dish makes a great accompaniment to the Kung Pao Chicken on page 96, or the Korean-style Pork Wraps on page 112. It's important to toss the spaghetti with the remaining peanut sauce just before serving, so the noodles won't soak up too much of the sauce. You can let the noodles chill in the refrigerator overnight before you toss with the second half of the dressing.

INGREDIENTS

1 pound spaghetti

4 tablespoons peanut oil

4 tablespoons creamy peanut butter

4 tablespoons soy sauce

2 teaspoons toasted sesame oil

2 tablespoons light brown sugar

2 teaspoons minced fresh ginger

1 to 2 pinches of crushed red pepper

¼ cup green onion tops, sliced diagonally

¼ cup chopped unsalted peanuts

TOOLS

Measuring cups and spoons • cutting board • chef's knife • vegetable peeler • medium soup pot or Dutch oven • oven mitts or pot holders • colander • large mixing bowl • medium mixing bowl • whisk • tongs • plastic wrap

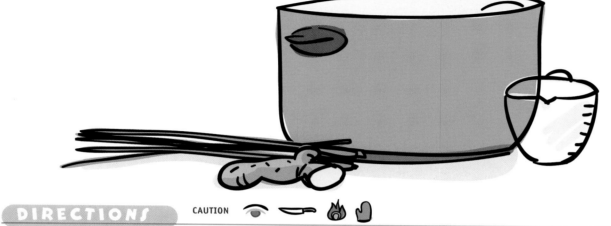

DIRECTIONS   CAUTION

1. Fill a medium soup pot or Dutch oven with water and bring to a boil over high heat.

2. Boil the pasta according to package directions, omitting salt, about 9 minutes or until al dente, not overcooked. "Al dente" is Italian for "to the tooth," meaning the pasta should offer a slight resistance when bitten.

3. Using oven mitts or pot holders, drain the spaghetti into a colander placed in a sink. Be careful to pour it away from you, so that the steam doesn't burn.

4. Place the spaghetti in a large mixing bowl and, using tongs, toss with 2 tablespoons of the peanut oil to keep the pasta from sticking. Set aside.

DID YOU KNOW . . .

It is said that Marco Polo brought pasta to Italy during his travels along the Silk Road in the thirteenth and fourteenth centuries. But there are records of pasta being eaten in Italy before that time. We know for sure that pasta has been a favorite all over the world for hundreds of years.

5. In a medium mixing bowl, whisk together the remaining peanut oil, peanut butter, soy sauce, sesame oil, brown sugar, ginger, and crushed red pepper. Whisk until smooth.

6. Pour half of the peanut mixture onto the spaghetti and, using tongs, toss to coat the pasta. Cover the spaghetti with plastic wrap and refrigerate until chilled, about 2 hours.

7. When ready to serve, pour the remaining peanut mixture onto the spaghetti and toss to coat the pasta. Sprinkle with sliced green onions and chopped peanuts. Serve immediately.

MEATBALL SOUP

Many cultures make meatball soup—but this one owes its flavors and heritage to the Italians. In certain parts of Italy, this soup is made to celebrate wedding festivities and is actually called Wedding Soup! Our version here is made hearty with the addition of tomatoes and pasta and is perfect for winter meals, especially when combined with some hot toasty bread and a salad.

INGREDIENTS

3/4 pound ground beef

1/4 pound ground pork

2 large eggs, lightly beaten

1/3 cup finely grated Parmesan cheese, plus more for garnish, if desired

1/4 cup Italian-style bread crumbs

1 tablespoon finely chopped garlic

1 teaspoon Emeril's Italian Essence or other dry Italian seasoning

1 teaspoon salt

2 pinches of crushed red pepper

2 tablespoons olive oil

1/2 cup chopped yellow onion

1/4 cup chopped celery

2 tablespoons tomato paste

1 (14.5-ounce) can whole tomatoes, crushed with your hands, with their juice

2 (14-ounce) cans reduced-sodium beef broth

1/2 cup ditalini or other small pasta shape for soups

3 cups water

2 tablespoons chopped fresh basil

TOOLS

Measuring cups and spoons • cutting board • chef's knife • box grater • medium mixing bowl • 2 plates • 4 1/2-quart soup pot or large saucepan • can opener • slotted spoon or tongs • wooden spoon • spoon • oven mitts or pot holders

DIRECTIONS

CAUTION

CAUTION Please follow the directions for handling raw meat on page 5 very carefully.

1. In a medium mixing bowl, combine the ground beef, ground pork, eggs, Parmesan cheese, bread crumbs, 2 teaspoons of the garlic, 3/4 teaspoon of the Italian Essence, 1/2 teaspoon of the salt, 1 pinch of crushed red pepper and, using clean hands, mix until thoroughly combined.

2. Using a tablespoon as your guide, divide the meat mixture into tablespoonfuls and roll into smooth balls with your hands. Set the rolled meatballs aside on a plate or other flat surface. Wash your hands.

STEP 2

3. In a 4 1/2-quart soup pot or large saucepan, heat the olive oil over medium-high heat until hot. Add half of the rolled meatballs and cook, turning occasionally with the tongs, until browned on all sides, about 4 minutes. Using a slotted spoon or tongs, remove the browned meatballs to a clean plate and set aside. Brown the remaining meatballs in the same manner and set aside.

4. Add the chopped onion and celery to the pot and cook, stirring with a wooden spoon, until the vegetables are soft, 3 to 4 minutes. Add the remaining teaspoon of minced garlic and cook for 1 minute. Add the tomato paste, crushed tomatoes and their juices, beef broth, water, remaining 1/4 teaspoon of Italian Essence, remaining 1/2 teaspoon of salt, remaining pinch of crushed red pepper, and stir to combine. Return the meatballs to the soup pot and bring the soup to a boil. Reduce the heat so that the soup just simmers and cook for 30 minutes.

5. Using a spoon, carefully skim any fat that has risen to the top of the soup and discard. Add the ditalini to the hot soup, stir well, and cook for 15 minutes, or until the pasta is cooked through. Stir in the chopped basil and serve the soup in wide bowls, garnished with additional grated Parmesan cheese, if desired.

EGG DROP SOUP

This soup is based on the Chinese version, but the Italians have one too! This may be one of the easiest soups to make, but just because it's quick doesn't mean it's not packed with flavor. The best part is that you can get creative with the vegetables that you add, such as snow peas or Chinese baby corn. When I'm not feeling well, this is the perfect soup to make me feel better.

DID YOU KNOW . . .

In an authentic Chinese meal, it is said that soup is often served as the last course because it allows the roast duck entrée to "swim" toward digestion.

INGREDIENTS

6 cups reduced-sodium chicken broth

6 to 8 large spinach leaves

½ cup green onions (about 4 small), sliced diagonally

4 shiitake mushrooms, stems removed, wiped clean, and thinly sliced

1 teaspoon soy sauce

Pinch of ground white pepper

2 large eggs, lightly beaten

TOOLS

Measuring cups and spoons • can opener (optional) • cutting board • chef's knife • medium saucepan or stockpot • fork or chopstick • ladle • oven mitts or pot holders

DIRECTIONS

CAUTION 👁 🔪 🔥 🧤 ✋

1. In a medium saucepan or stockpot, bring the chicken broth to a simmer.

2. Stack the spinach leaves on top of each other and roll them up tightly. Thinly slice into ribbonlike strips.

STEP 2

3. Add the spinach, 6 tablespoons of the sliced green onion, the mushrooms, soy sauce, and white pepper to the broth.

4. When the broth begins to simmer again, gradually add the beaten eggs in a slow and steady stream. Use a fork or a chopstick to stir the broth—this will shred the eggs into ribbons as they cook.

STEP 4

5. Cook the soup for 1 minute more and remove from the heat.

6. Ladle the soup into bowls and garnish with remaining 2 tablespoons of sliced green onion. Serve hot.

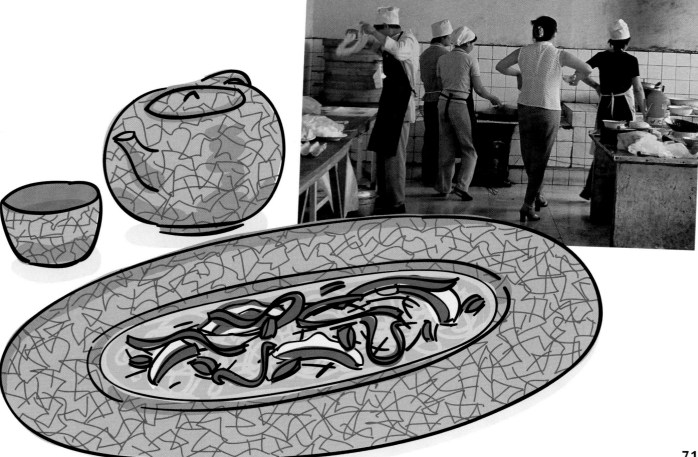

THAI COCONUT SOUP WITH CHICKEN AND SHRIMP

Lemongrass is important in Thai cooking, and the flavors in this soup are amazing! The sweet coconut milk with the tangy lime juice and a hint of chili spice all make this soup a frenzy of flavors. If you can find fresh Thai basil leaves, substitute them for the cilantro for a truly authentic taste of Thailand.

INGREDIENTS

½ pound boneless, skinless chicken breasts, cut into bite-size pieces

¼ teaspoon salt

¼ teaspoon ground black pepper

½ pound shrimp, peeled and deveined (page 17)

¼ teaspoon Emeril's Original Essence

3½ cups reduced-sodium chicken broth

2 tablespoons fish sauce

2 teaspoons minced fresh ginger

1 tablespoon minced garlic

1 (5-inch) piece lemongrass, cut in half lengthwise and crushed with edge of knife (see Tip)

1 (13.5-ounce) can coconut milk

1 cup quartered button mushrooms, stems removed

½ teaspoon crushed red pepper

½ cup snow peas

3 tablespoons fresh lime juice

2 tablespoons chopped fresh cilantro

TOOLS

Measuring cups and spoons • cutting board • chef's knife • vegetable peeler (optional) • can opener • juicer (optional) • 2 small mixing bowls • large soup pot or Dutch oven • wooden spoon • ladle • oven mitts or pot holders

DIRECTIONS

CAUTION

1. Place the chicken in a small mixing bowl and season with the salt and pepper. Set aside.

   CAUTION: Please follow the directions for handling raw meat on page 5 very carefully.

2. Season the shrimp in a separate small mixing bowl with Essence and set aside.

3. Combine the chicken broth, fish sauce, ginger, garlic, and lemongrass in a large soup pot or Dutch oven. Bring to a boil over high heat. Reduce the heat to medium-low and simmer for 10 minutes.

4. Add the diced, seasoned chicken, coconut milk, mushrooms, and crushed red pepper. Simmer 10 minutes.

5. Add the seasoned shrimp, snow peas, and lime juice. Simmer an additional 3 to 4 minutes, or until the shrimp are pink and cooked through and the chicken is cooked through.

6. Using oven mitts or pot holders, remove from the heat and stir in the chopped cilantro.

7. Remove and discard the lemongrass before serving the soup.

TIP

When using lemongrass, remove the grassy tops and any hard root section. Using the blunt edge of a knife or a heavy pot, bruise the stalk all over. (Be careful not to pulverize the stalk or it will fall apart during cooking.)

DID YOU KNOW . . .

Lemongrass is popular throughout Southeast Asia, and not just for cooking. The long stalks are sometimes dipped in scented water and brushed on the body to keep mosquitoes away.

MEXICAN TORTILLA SOUP
(tohr-TEE-yuh)

The refreshing flavors of this soup remind me of summer, but the spiciness from the jalapeño makes it great for any time of the year.

I like to garnish it with shredded cheese, avocado, sour cream, and a little extra cilantro to kick things up. You'll have fun crushing up the tortilla chips, too!

DID YOU KNOW . . .

The jalapeño pepper has been used in cooking throughout Mexico since the time of the Aztecs. It's used now in jelly, ketchup, mustard, and even added to chocolate for an an extra dessert kick!

INGREDIENTS

1 pound boneless, skinless chicken breasts, cut into bite-size pieces

½ teaspoon salt

½ teaspoon ground black pepper

1 tablespoon olive oil

1 cup diced yellow onion

½ cup diced green bell pepper

1 tablespoon minced garlic

½ small jalapeño, stemmed, seeded, and finely chopped (about 2 teaspoons)

4½ cups reduced-sodium chicken broth

1 teaspoon ground cumin

½ teaspoon ground coriander

3 tablespoons fresh lime juice

1 tablespoon chopped fresh cilantro, plus extra for garnish

1 cup chopped tomatoes (2 to 3 small Roma tomatoes)

Crushed tortilla chips

1 ripe avocado, peeled, pit removed, and diced (optional)

Sour cream (optional)

Cheddar cheese, grated (optional)

TOOLS

Measuring cups and spoons • cutting board • chef's knife • rubber gloves • juicer (optional) • medium stockpot or Dutch oven • wooden spoon • ladle • oven mitts or pot holders • grater (optional) • can opener (optional)

DIRECTIONS

CAUTION

1. Season the chicken with salt and pepper and set aside.

   CAUTION Please follow the directions for handling raw meat on page 5 very carefully.

2. Heat the olive oil in a medium stockpot or Dutch oven over medium-high heat. Add the onion and bell pepper and cook, stirring, 2 to 3 minutes, or until the vegetables are softened.

3. Add the garlic and jalapeño and sauté for 1 minute, stirring constantly.

   CAUTION Always handle jalapeño peppers with rubber gloves and be careful not to touch your eyes or skin.

4. Add the chicken and cook, stirring occasionally, for about 2 minutes. The chicken will brown slightly.

5. Stir in the chicken broth, cumin, coriander, and lime juice.

6. Bring the soup to a boil, and reduce the heat to medium-low. Allow the soup to simmer for 5 minutes.

7. Stir in the cilantro and tomatoes and simmer an additional 5 minutes.

8. Place about ½ cup crushed tortilla chips in each serving bowl. Ladle the hot soup over the tortillas and garnish with a little extra cilantro, diced avocado, sour cream, and grated cheese, as you prefer.

PORTUGUESE POTATO DUMPLING SOUP

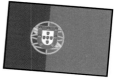

Of course I had to include some recipes from my own Portuguese heritage! This soup is filled with dumplings that are so good, you can make them for a snack all by themselves. Just sauté the dumplings until golden and enjoy. If you're looking for a richer flavor, you can use beef broth in place of the water and chicken broth. But any way you try it, you'll be amazed!

DIRECTIONS   CAUTION

1. Wash the potatoes and place in a small saucepan. Cover with cold water and 1 teaspoon of the salt and bring to a boil over high heat. Reduce the heat to medium-low and simmer for 30 to 35 minutes until the potatoes are tender. Drain.

INGREDIENTS

2 large baking potatoes (about 1¾ pounds)

2 teaspoons salt

2 to 3 ounces diced ham, ground in a food processor to equal ⅓ cup

½ cup grated Parmesan cheese

2 large eggs, lightly beaten

2 tablespoons unsalted butter

¼ teaspoon ground freshly grated nutmeg

1 cup all-purpose flour

2½ cups reduced-sodium beef broth

2 cups reduced-sodium chicken broth

1½ cups water

1 cup diced yellow onion

1 cup peeled, sliced carrots

1 tablespoon chopped fresh parsley

6 tablespoons vegetable oil

TOOLS

Measuring cups and spoons • cutting board • chef's knife • small saucepan • vegetable peeler • food processor • ricer • small colander (optional) • medium mixing bowl • spoon or rubber spatula • box grater • small baking sheet • 2 small mixing bowls • paper towels • 6-quart soup pot or stockpot with lid • can opener (optional) • large nonstick skillet • ladle • plate (optional) • oven mitts or pot holders

2. Peel the potatoes while they are still warm. (Not too hot, or you might burn your hands.) Place the peeled potatoes in a ricer over a small bowl and push through. Alternatively, using the back of a spoon or a rubber spatula, mash the potatoes through the holes in a colander into a bowl set below it. You can mash the potatoes by hand, but the dumplings won't be as fluffy.

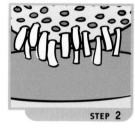

STEP 2

3. Add the ham, Parmesan cheese, beaten eggs, butter, nutmeg, and the remaining 1 teaspoon of salt to the mashed potatoes. Mix well to combine.

4. Line a small baking sheet with paper towels and place the flour in a small mixing bowl.

5. Roll the potato mixture into little balls, about 2 rounded teaspoonfuls each. Toss each dumpling in the flour, shake off the excess, and place on the prepared baking sheet. Set aside.

6. In a 6-quart soup pot or stockpot, combine the beef broth, chicken broth, water, onion, carrots, and parsley. Bring to a boil and boil for 10 minutes. Turn off the heat and cover to keep warm.

7. Heat 2 tablespoons of the oil in a large nonstick skillet over medium to medium-high heat. Add one-third of the potato dumplings to the skillet, leaving enough room to turn them. Brown the dumplings on all sides, 6 to 8 minutes, until golden, and transfer with a ladle to a paper towel–lined plate or baking sheet. Continue to brown the remaining dumplings, using 2 tablespoons of oil for each batch.

8. Heat the beef-chicken stock over medium-high heat until simmering. Using a ladle, carefully place the dumplings into the simmering stock. Simmer the dumplings for 3 to 5 minutes. Serve immediately since the dumplings are fragile.

CROQUE MONSIEUR

(KROHK muhs-YOOR)

In France, this sandwich is as popular as a simple grilled cheese is in America—but you'll see that the French really know how to dress things up! This grilled sandwich is kicked way up by the addition of béchamel sauce and grated Gruyère cheese. Then the whole thing is broiled briefly so that it becomes hot, crunchy, and bubbly and—oh, baby, don't make me talk about it! This is definitely food of love!

DID YOU KNOW . . .

The French translation of this sandwich is roughly "crunchy sir," maybe because it becomes crispy when broiled. A Croque Madame has a fried egg on top.

INGREDIENTS

3 tablespoons unsalted butter

2 tablespoons all-purpose flour

$^3/_4$ cup whole milk

$^1/_8$ teaspoon salt

$^1/_8$ teaspoon ground white pepper

Pinch of ground nutmeg

8 slices thin white sandwich bread

2 teaspoons Dijon mustard

2 ounces very thinly sliced ham (about 4 thin slices)

2 ounces thinly sliced Gruyère cheese

$^1/_4$ cup grated Gruyère cheese

2 teaspoons chopped fresh chives for garnish (optional)

TOOLS

Measuring cups and spoons • cutting board • chef's knife • small saucepan with lid • wooden spoon • whisk • butter knife • large skillet • metal spatula • small baking sheet • spoon • box grater • oven mitts or pot holders

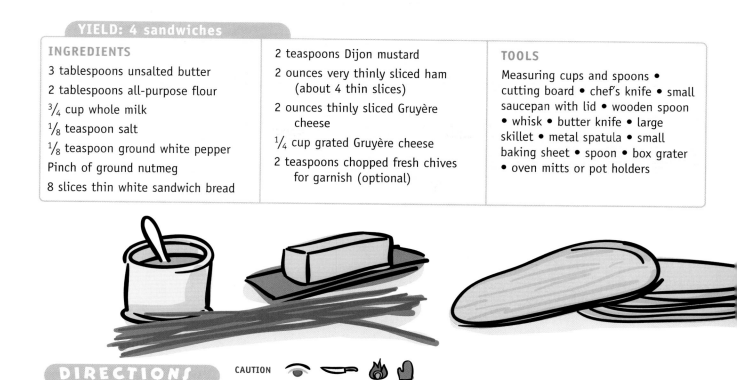

DIRECTIONS   CAUTION

1. To prepare the béchamel sauce, melt 2 tablespoons of the butter in a small saucepan over medium heat. Add the flour and stir for 1 minute, until bubbly. Do not allow to brown. Add the milk $^1/_4$ cup at a time, whisking to combine each addition with the butter mixture. Increase the heat to medium-high and cook, whisking constantly, until the sauce thickens, about 2 minutes. Season with the salt, white pepper, and nutmeg and set aside, covered, while you prepare the sandwiches.

2. Preheat the broiler.

CAUTION Please have an adult help you to use your broiler.

3. Place 4 of the bread slices on a work surface. Spread one side of each slice with $^1/_2$ teaspoon of the Dijon mustard. Divide the ham and Gruyère slices evenly among the 4 bread slices. Top each sandwich with the remaining 4 slices of bread. Lightly butter the outsides of each sandwich with the remaining tablespoon of butter.

STEP 3

4. Heat a large skillet over medium-low heat. When hot, add the buttered sandwiches to the skillet and cook until they are golden brown on both sides, about 2 minutes per side.

5. Using a metal spatula, transfer the sandwiches to a small baking sheet. Divide the béchamel sauce evenly among the tops of the sandwiches and, using the back of a spoon, spread the sauce so that it covers most of the sandwich tops. Then sprinkle the grated Gruyère evenly over the sauce. Using oven mitts or pot holders, transfer the baking sheet to the oven and broil the sandwiches until the sauce is bubbly and the cheese is lightly browned in spots, about 2 to 3 minutes.

6. Using oven mitts or pot holders, remove the sandwiches from the oven and garnish with chives, if desired. Serve immediately.

PAN BAGNA (pan BAHN-yah)

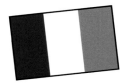

This is how they like to eat tuna sandwiches in the south of France—and once you try it, you'll know why! They use the wonderful produce available there—olives, capers, tomatoes, olive oil, fresh basil—for a tuna sandwich that is nothing like the American version. In France, they press the sandwiches slightly after making them so that all of the juices mingle and seep into the bread. Oh, baby!

INGREDIENTS

3 tablespoons red wine vinegar

2 tablespoons capers, undrained

1 teaspoon minced garlic

1 teaspoon Dijon mustard

½ teaspoon salt

¼ teaspoon freshly ground black pepper

½ cup extra-virgin olive oil

4 (6-inch) French bread rolls or other crusty buns or rolls, such as sourdough or Italian

2 (6-ounce) cans solid white tuna packed in water, drained and flaked

2 small tomatoes, thinly sliced (6 to 8 ounces)

½ green or red bell pepper, cut into thin strips

⅓ cup coarsely chopped Kalamata olives

2 to 3 cups mixed greens

8 large fresh basil leaves, coarsely chopped

TOOLS

Measuring cups and spoons • cutting board • chef's knife • small nonreactive bowl • whisk • can opener • serrated bread knife • medium mixing bowl • large spatula (optional) • plastic wrap (optional)

DIRECTIONS   CAUTION

1. In a small nonreactive bowl, whisk together the vinegar, capers, garlic, mustard, salt, and pepper. Add the olive oil and whisk to combine. Set the vinaigrette aside while you assemble the remaining sandwich ingredients.

2. Using a serrated bread knife, cut each sandwich roll in half lengthwise. If the bread is very dense and doughy, use your fingers to pull out some of the doughy interior, leaving a ½-inch shell on both the top and the bottom portions of each roll.

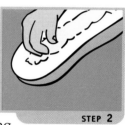

STEP 2

3. Drizzle 2 tablespoons of the vinaigrette over the insides of each roll, 1 tablespoon for the top and 1 for the bottom. Divide the tuna evenly among the bottom portions of each roll. Divide the tomato slices evenly over the tuna. Divide the bell pepper slices evenly over the tomato slices, and then divide the olives evenly among the sandwiches.

4. In a medium mixing bowl, toss the mixed greens with 1 tablespoon of the remaining vinaigrette and top each sandwich with some of the greens. Drizzle any remaining vinaigrette and scatter the basil leaves over the sandwiches and place each sandwich top over the filling. Press down on each sandwich with your hands or with a large spatula to compress slightly.

5. Cut each sandwich in half and serve, or wrap in plastic wrap and refrigerate for up to 6 hours before serving.

Note: This sandwich could also be done on one long baguette and then sliced into serving pieces.

SUPER-STUFFED BURRITOS
(ber-ee-tohs)

Burrito means "little donkey" in Spanish, and it is a favorite Mexican dish, especially in the U.S. These small but super-packed burritos are fantastic—with rice and beans, cheese, salsa, and sour cream—but feel free to kick yours up by adding any other favorite ingredients. Leftover roast chicken or meat, cut into bite-size pieces, makes a wonderful addition, as do roast veggies or cooked spinach. Or, try a dollop of guacamole or cubed avocado. Make it your way!

INGREDIENTS

2 tablespoons vegetable oil

$\frac{1}{2}$ cup chopped yellow onion

$\frac{1}{4}$ cup chopped green bell pepper

1 teaspoon minced garlic

$\frac{3}{4}$ teaspoon salt

$\frac{1}{4}$ teaspoon ground cumin

$\frac{1}{4}$ teaspoon dried oregano

$\frac{1}{2}$ cup long-grain white rice

1 cup water

1 (15-ounce) can black beans, drained and rinsed

8 (8-inch) flour tortillas

1 cup grated Monterey Jack, Pepper Jack, or Cheddar cheese

$1\frac{1}{2}$ cups ranchero salsa (page 36) or your favorite store-bought salsa

1 cup sour cream

$\frac{1}{4}$ cup chopped fresh cilantro (optional)

Bottled hot sauce (optional)

TOOLS

Measuring cups and spoons • cutting board • chef's knife • medium saucepan with lid • wooden spoon • can opener • strainer • spoon • box grater • oven mitts or pot holders

---

DIRECTIONS

CAUTION

1. In a medium saucepan, heat the oil over medium-high heat until hot. Add the chopped onion and bell pepper and cook until the vegetables are soft, about 4 minutes. Add the garlic, salt, cumin, and oregano, and cook for 1 minute, stirring constantly. Add the rice and cook, stirring, until fragrant, about 2 minutes.

2. Add the water and drained beans and bring to a boil. Stir well, reduce the heat to low, and cover the saucepan. Cook for 20 minutes, undisturbed, until the rice is tender and has absorbed all of the liquid. Remove from the heat and let stand, undisturbed, for 5 minutes before serving.

3. Heat the flour tortillas according to package directions—the microwave works well for this if you have one available.

4. Fill each warm tortilla with a heaping $\frac{1}{3}$ cup of the cooked rice and bean mixture placed in a line down the center of each tortilla. Top each mound of rice with 2 tablespoons of the grated cheese and roll the bottom side of the tortilla over the filling. Fold both of the side edges up over the filling, then roll the tortilla to form a cylinder shape.

STEP 4

5. Spoon 3 tablespoons of salsa over the top of each burrito and then top each with 2 tablespoons of the sour cream. Garnish each burrito with $\frac{1}{2}$ tablespoon of chopped cilantro and serve with hot sauce, if desired.

STEP 4

CUBAN SANDWICH

It's believed this sandwich originated in Florida, where there is a large Cuban immigrant population. It's another example of the excellent cooking brought over from other countries. You can also use leftover meat from the Puerto Rican Pork Roast on page 122 to make this sandwich. Any way you make it, it's good!

DIRECTIONS   CAUTION 👁 🔪 🔥 🧤 👐

1. Position rack in center of oven and preheat the oven to 400°F.

2. Sprinkle the pork tenderloin with ¾ teaspoon of the salt and the pepper.

INGREDIENTS

1 (1-pound) pork tenderloin, trimmed of any fat or tough membranes

1 teaspoon kosher salt

1/2 teaspoon ground black pepper

1 tablespoon olive oil

4 garlic cloves, unpeeled

1/2 cup mayonnaise

1 1/2 teaspoons fresh lime juice

1/4 teaspoon plus 1 pinch of ground cumin

4 individual Cuban bread loaves or 1 loaf Cuban or French bread, cut into 4 sections

12 very thin slices smoked ham

8 thin slices Swiss cheese

12 slices dill pickle

4 tablespoons unsalted butter

TOOLS

Measuring cups and spoons • cutting board • chef's knife • medium ovenproof skillet (no plastic or wooden handles) • meat thermometer • oven mitts or pot holders • tongs • juicer (optional) • small mixing bowl • serrated bread knife • medium nonstick skillet or griddle • large metal spatula • plate

3. Heat the olive oil in a medium ovenproof skillet over high heat. Carefully add the tenderloin to the oil and sear on all sides until golden brown, about 5 minutes. Add the unpeeled garlic cloves to the skillet and place the skillet in the oven. Bake for 17 to 20 minutes, or until the pork is cooked through and a meat thermometer inserted into the thickest portion of the meat registers 160°F.

CAUTION: Please follow the directions for cooking pork on page 26 very carefully.

4. Using oven mitts or pot holders, remove the skillet from the oven. Carefully remove the pork and the garlic cloves from the skillet and allow to rest, undisturbed, on a clean cutting board for 10 minutes.

5. In a small mixing bowl, combine the mayonnaise, lime juice, cumin, and remaining 1/4 teaspoon salt. Stir to combine.

6. When the garlic cloves have cooled slightly, squeeze the pulp from the insides of the cloves into the mayonnaise mixture, and discard the outer husks. Mix well.

7. Slice the pork diagonally into thin, 1/4-inch slices.

8. Using a serrated bread knife, slice the bread loaves in half horizontally.

9. Smear about 2 tablespoons of the mayonnaise mixture onto each sandwich bottom. Top with 3 to 4 slices of pork and 3 thin slices of ham. Place 2 slices of cheese and 3 dill pickle slices on top of the meat. Top each with the other sandwich half.

STEP 6

STEP 7

10. In a medium nonstick skillet or a griddle, heat 1 tablespoon of the butter over medium heat. Place 1 sandwich in the melted butter and carefully press the top of the sandwich into the skillet using a large metal spatula. Be careful when using metal on a nonstick skillet, as it can scratch the surface. Cook until browned, about 2 to 3 minutes. Using the spatula, turn the sandwich and cook an additional 2 to 3 minutes until golden, pressing with the spatula to flatten. Remove to a plate and keep warm.

11. Continue with the remaining sandwiches and butter. Serve the sandwiches warm.

PEPPERONI AND FRESH MOZZARELLA PANINI (pah-NEE-nee)

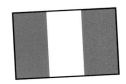

Panini is the Italian word for rolls or biscuits—but now it also means a small Italian sandwich, grilled or not, filled with a variety of meats, vegetables, and/or cheeses. Our version makes a great sandwich to serve alongside a bowl of soup for a filling lunch or dinner. Or, make these sandwiches and cut them into small strips or pieces for your family's next party. Be sure you don't skip the oil-and-vinegar dressing—this is what really makes the sandwich come alive!

DID YOU KNOW . . .

Bocconcini is Italian for "little mouthfuls." These little mozzarella balls are just the right size to pop in your mouth whole.

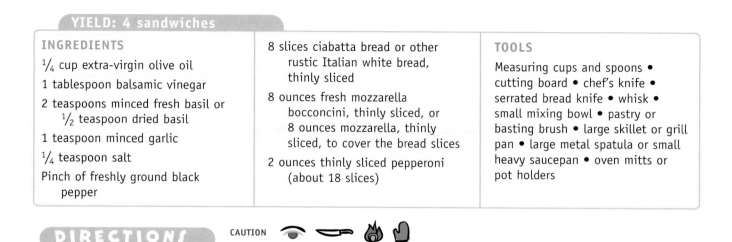

INGREDIENTS

¼ cup extra-virgin olive oil

1 tablespoon balsamic vinegar

2 teaspoons minced fresh basil or ½ teaspoon dried basil

1 teaspoon minced garlic

¼ teaspoon salt

Pinch of freshly ground black pepper

8 slices ciabatta bread or other rustic Italian white bread, thinly sliced

8 ounces fresh mozzarella bocconcini, thinly sliced, or 8 ounces mozzarella, thinly sliced, to cover the bread slices

2 ounces thinly sliced pepperoni (about 18 slices)

TOOLS

Measuring cups and spoons • cutting board • chef's knife • serrated bread knife • whisk • small mixing bowl • pastry or basting brush • large skillet or grill pan • large metal spatula or small heavy saucepan • oven mitts or pot holders

DIRECTIONS   CAUTION

1. Whisk 3 tablespoons of the olive oil, vinegar, basil, garlic, salt, and pepper in a small mixing bowl to blend. Set the vinaigrette aside.

2. Arrange the slices of bread on a flat work surface and, using a pastry or basting brush, brush one side of each slice with the vinaigrette, dividing it equally.

3. Divide the mozzarella equally among 4 of the bread slices. Top the mozzarella with the pepperoni slices, then place the remaining 4 slices of bread on top of the mozzarella and pepperoni, brushed sides down, to form 4 sandwiches.

4. Brush the outsides of each sandwich lightly with some of the remaining tablespoon of olive oil.

5. Heat a large skillet or grill pan over medium heat. When the skillet is hot, add the sandwiches and cook until the bread is golden brown and the cheese is melted, pressing occasionally with a large metal spatula or the bottom of a small heavy saucepan, 4 to 5 minutes per side. Serve hot.

B.L.T. HOT DOGS

 Two of my favorite All-American foods are hot dogs and bacon, lettuce, and tomato sandwiches. This recipe combines the best of both worlds! If you really want a treat, try making the homemade hot dog buns on page 158. What could be better for a summer barbecue?

DID YOU KNOW . . .

A hot dog is a sausage. Sausages may be the oldest form of processed food and were mentioned in Homer's Odyssey in the ninth century B.C!

INGREDIENTS		TOOLS
8 hot dogs (organic, all-beef hot dogs recommended)	8 hot dog buns	Measuring cup • cutting board • chef's knife • small baking sheet • oven mitts or pot holders
8 regular thin-cut bacon slices	1 cup diced tomatoes (about 2 small tomatoes)	
8 iceberg lettuce leaves	Mustard	
	Mayonnaise	

DIRECTIONS   CAUTION

1. Position rack in center of oven and preheat the oven to 375°F.

2. Wrap each hot dog with a slice of bacon, tucking both edges under so that the bacon does not come unwrapped during baking.

3. Place the hot dogs on a small baking sheet. Bake for 40 to 45 minutes, until the bacon is crispy and well browned. Using oven mitts or pot holders, remove the baking sheet from the oven.

4. Stack the lettuce leaves on top of each other and roll up tightly. Thinly slice into ribbonlike strips.

5. Place one hot dog in each bun and top with diced tomatoes and lettuce.

6. Serve with mustard and mayonnaise or other desired condiments.

STEP 4

MAIN-MEAL MASTERPIECES

LINGUINE BOLOGNESE

(lihn-GWEE-nee baw-law-NYEH-seh)

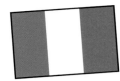

This pasta dish has a rich, meaty sauce that takes its name from the city of Bologna in the northern part of Italy, not far from the capital of Rome. Try it over any pasta that you love—fettucine, spaghetti, capellini—you name it! The sauce takes 1½ hours to cook, but it's worth it!

INGREDIENTS

6 ounces bacon or pancetta, diced

1½ cups chopped yellow onion

1¼ cups finely chopped carrots

¾ cup finely chopped celery

¾ teaspoon salt

½ teaspoon freshly ground black
pepper

1½ pounds ground chuck

4 teaspoons white wine vinegar

1½ tablespoons minced garlic

⅓ cup tomato paste

3 cups reduced-sodium beef broth

1¼ cups whole milk

¼ cup heavy cream

½ pound linguine pasta, prepared
according to package directions

Finely grated Parmesan cheese
(optional)

TOOLS

Measuring cups and spoons •
cutting board • chef's knife •
medium saucepan with lid • can
opener (optional) • wooden spoon
• small mixing bowl • large
heatproof bowl • box grater
(optional)

DIRECTIONS   CAUTION

1. In a medium saucepan over medium-high heat, cook the bacon until it is crisp and has released almost all of its fat, about 6 minutes. This is called rendering.

2. Add the onion, carrots, celery, salt, and pepper and cook, stirring frequently, until the vegetables are very soft and lightly browned around the edges, about 6 minutes.

3. Add the ground chuck and cook, stirring to break up any clumps, until the meat is browned, about 5 minutes.

4. Add the vinegar, garlic, and tomato paste and cook for 2 minutes, stirring constantly.

5. Add the beef broth and bring to a boil. Lower the heat so that the sauce just simmers. Simmer, partially covered, for 15 minutes.

6. Combine the milk and cream in a small mixing bowl. After the sauce has simmered for 15 minutes, and at even intervals, start adding the milk-cream mixture little by little—¼ cup or so at a time over 1½ hours. By the end of the 1½ hours, the milk mixture should be completely incorporated and the sauce should be very thick and creamy. This sauce is not supposed to be very "saucy"—it should be tender morsels of meat coated by a thick, creamy sauce.

7. Transfer the cooked pasta to a large heatproof bowl and add the sauce. Toss the pasta with the sauce and serve immediately, garnished with grated Parmesan cheese, if desired.

BEEF STROGANOFF

(STROH-guh-noff)

 This world-renowned dish is named after a Russian diplomat, Count Pavel Stroganov, and is a simple sauté of tender beef strips, onions, and mushrooms in a creamy sauce. I like mine with egg noodles, as seen here, but it's equally at home with a simple rice pilaf, if you prefer.

INGREDIENTS

2 tablespoons olive oil

1 pound beef sirloin,
    cut into 2 x 1 x ½-inch strips

1 tablespoon plus 1 teaspoon salt

¾ teaspoon freshly ground black
    pepper, plus more for seasoning
    noodles

5 tablespoons unsalted butter

12 ounces mushrooms, quartered

1½ cups thinly sliced yellow onion

1 tablespoon tomato paste

2 tablespoons all-purpose flour

1 (14-ounce) can reduced-sodium
    beef broth

5 tablespoons sour cream

2 teaspoons Dijon mustard

1 (12-ounce) package wide egg
    noodles

1 tablespoon chopped parsley

TOOLS

Measuring cups and spoons •
cutting board • chef's knife •
tongs • large plate • can opener
(optional) • wooden spoon • large
12-inch skillet with lid • whisk •
large pot • colander

DIRECTIONS

CAUTION

1. Heat a large 12-inch skillet over medium-high heat and add the olive oil.

2. Season the beef strips with 1 teaspoon of the salt and ½ teaspoon of the pepper. Add the beef to the hot pan and sear for 1 to 2 minutes, then turn with tongs onto the second side. Continue to sear the meat on the second side for another minute, or until golden brown. Transfer the beef to a large plate.

3. Return the skillet to the heat and add 3 tablespoons of the butter to the pan. When the butter has melted, add the mushrooms and sauté, stirring often, until the mushrooms are well browned, about 7 minutes. Add the onion to the pan and cook, stirring often, until the onion is very soft and lightly browned around the edges, about 4 to 5 minutes. Add the tomato paste to the pan and cook, stirring, for 1 minute. Whisk in the flour and cook, stirring, for another minute. Add the beef broth and beef to the pan and bring the contents of the pan to a boil while whisking constantly.

4. Remove from the heat, then whisk in the sour cream and mustard. Set aside, covered and off the heat, while you prepare the noodles.

5. Bring a large pot of water to a boil, add the remaining 1 tablespoon of salt, and cook the noodles until al dente (see page 65), about 7 to 8 minutes. Drain the cooked noodles in a colander in the sink and return them to the pot. Add the remaining 2 tablespoons of butter to the noodles and season to taste with black pepper. Toss to blend.

6. Reheat the Beef Stroganoff gently over medium heat, stirring frequently. Add the parsley and stir to combine. Do not allow the sauce to boil.

7. Once the beef is hot, divide the noodles among 4 dinner plates and top with the sauce. Serve immediately.

KUNG PAO CHICKEN
(kuhng pow)

There are several ideas for how this chicken dish was named. Some say it was for a Chinese general who accidentally knocked a jar of chiles into his chicken stir-fry. It sure has become a spicy favorite all over the world! Since the chicken and vegetables are cut small and sautéed at very high heat in a small amount of oil, this meal is ready in no time. If you don't like it as spicy as I do, just choose the amount of pepper that's right for you.

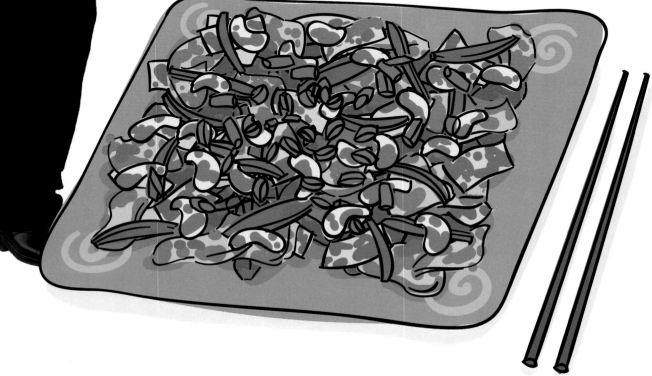

INGREDIENTS

Marinade:

1 pound boneless, skinless chicken breasts, cut into thin strips, 3 to 4 inches long

2 tablespoons rice vinegar

2 tablespoons peanut or vegetable oil

2 tablespoons soy sauce

2 tablespoons hoisin sauce

2 tablespoons cornstarch

1/4 teaspoon salt

Sauce:

5 tablespoons reduced-sodium chicken broth

2 tablespoons soy sauce

2 tablespoons rice vinegar

2 teaspoons sugar

1 tablespoon hoisin sauce

1 tablespoon cornstarch

2 tablespoons peanut or vegetable oil

1 (1/2-inch) piece fresh ginger, peeled, sliced, and smashed

1 1/2 tablespoons minced garlic

1/4 to 1/2 teaspoon crushed red pepper

3 green onions, sliced diagonally, bottom and top parts separated

1 (8-ounce) can bamboo shoots, drained

1 small red bell pepper, seeded and julienned

1/3 cup unsalted roasted cashews or peanuts

Steamed white rice, for serving

TOOLS

Measuring cups and spoons • cutting board • chef's knife • can opener • medium mixing bowl • plastic wrap • 2 small mixing bowls • whisk • vegetable peeler • large skillet • wooden spoon or tongs • oven mitts or pot holders

DIRECTIONS CAUTION

1. In a medium mixing bowl, combine the chicken strips and the ingredients for the marinade. Cover with plastic wrap and refrigerate for 20 to 30 minutes.

   CAUTION | Please follow the directions for handling raw poultry on page 5 very carefully.

2. For the sauce, combine 3 tablespoons of the chicken broth, soy sauce, rice vinegar, sugar, and hoisin sauce in a small mixing bowl. Set aside.

3. Combine the remaining 2 tablespoons of chicken broth and the cornstarch in another small mixing bowl, whisking to combine. Set aside.

4. Heat the oil in a large skillet over high heat. Carefully add the ginger and garlic and cook, stirring constantly, for 30 seconds. (When stir-frying, the oil should be very hot, but not smoking. Be careful that it doesn't splash out of the skillet while stirring.)

5. Add the crushed red pepper and the chicken, discarding the extra marinade. Cook, stirring, for about 3 minutes.

6. Add the green onion bottoms, the bamboo shoots, and the red bell pepper. Cook an additional minute, stirring constantly.

7. Stir in the chicken broth–soy sauce mixture and bring to a boil.

8. Add the chicken broth–cornstarch mixture and cook, stirring until the sauce boils and thickens. Add the cashews or peanuts and stir to coat.

9. Remove from the heat and garnish with green onion tops. Serve hot over steamed rice.

SHRIMP TERIYAKI

(tehr-uh-YAH-kee)

Of all the Japanese dishes that have made their way into the hearts of Americans, teriyaki is one of the most loved. Whether it's made with beef, chicken, shrimp, or pork, you can count on anything cooked teriyaki-style to be marinated in soy sauce that has been combined with sugar and other ingredients and then cooked quickly to seal in juices for a delicious flavor and texture. Homemade teriyaki sauce is extra special, but if you are short on time you can use store-bought.

DIRECTIONS

CAUTION

1. Place the shrimp in a large nonreactive bowl and add the teriyaki sauce. Stir to combine well and allow to marinate, refrigerated, for 20 minutes.

2. After 20 minutes, remove the shrimp from the refrigerator and strain in a colander set over a clean bowl. Reserve the teriyaki sauce and the shrimp separately.

INGREDIENTS		TOOLS
1 pound medium shrimp (21 to 25 per pound), peeled and deveined (page 17) 3/4 cup Homemade Teriyaki Sauce (recipe follows) or store-bought 2 tablespoons peanut oil 1/2 cup diced yellow onion	1/2 cup diced red bell pepper 1/2 cup carrot, sliced into 1/8-inch rounds 2 teaspoons chopped fresh cilantro Steamed white rice, for serving	Measuring cups and spoons • cutting board • paring knife • chef's knife • wooden spoon • 2 large nonreactive bowls • colander • large 12-inch skillet • tongs • platter • oven mitts or pot holders

3. Heat a large 12-inch skillet over medium-high heat and add 1 tablespoon of the peanut oil to the pan. Once the oil is hot, add the shrimp to the pan and sear for 1 minute. Using tongs, turn the shrimp over and sear for an additional minute on the other side. Remove the shrimp from the pan and place on a platter.

DID YOU KNOW . . .

Japanese cooking is known for its simplicity and is rooted in Buddhist influences. Japanese meals were often structured to include five flavors (sweet, spicy, salty, bitter, and sour) and five colors (yellow, black, white, green, and red).

4. Add the remaining tablespoon of peanut oil to the pan along with the onion, red bell pepper, and carrot. Sauté, stirring frequently, until the onion is soft and lightly caramelized, about 3 to 4 minutes.

5. Return the shrimp to the pan, along with the reserved teriyaki sauce, and increase the heat to high.

6. Continue to cook and reduce the teriyaki sauce with the shrimp and vegetables, stirring often, until the sauce is thick and glazes the shrimp, about 4 to 5 minutes.

7. Add the chopped cilantro to the pan and toss to blend. Serve the shrimp with steamed white rice.

HOMEMADE TERIYAKI SAUCE

INGREDIENTS		TOOLS
1/2 cup light soy sauce 1/4 cup mirin sauce 2 tablespoons sugar 2 tablespoons peanut oil	1/2 teaspoon sesame oil 1 tablespoon minced garlic 1 tablespoon minced fresh ginger 1 tablespoon minced green onion, white part only	Measuring cups and spoons • cutting board • chef's knife • blender • airtight container (optional)

DIRECTIONS   CAUTION

1. Place all of the ingredients in a blender and process on low for 1 minute, until the ingredients are well incorporated.

2. Use immediately or store in an airtight container in the refrigerator for up to 3 days.

JAMAICAN JERKED CHICKEN WITH BARBECUE SAUCE

This spicy way of flavoring food is called "jerk" in Jamaica. They usually use a very hot little pepper called a Scotch bonnet to give their food its kick. I use jalapeños when I make this at home, but if you're feeling adventurous, try the Scotch bonnet instead. You have to start preparing this the night before, but it's well worth it! Serve the chicken with some white rice and you've got yourself a Jamaican meal!

DIRECTIONS

CAUTION

1. Place the chicken thighs in a medium mixing bowl and pour in 2 cups of the vinegar. Rub the vinegar into the chicken with your clean hands and drain.

2. Rinse the chicken in cold water and pat dry with paper towels. Place chicken inside a large resealable plastic food storage bag and set aside. Wash hands again thoroughly before proceeding.

3. For the marinade: In the bowl of a food processor, combine the remaining teaspoon of vinegar, the green onions, jalapeños, soy sauce, Kitchen Bouquet, lime juice, allspice, bay leaves, garlic, salt, sugar, thyme, and cinnamon. Process until smooth, stopping to scrape down the sides of the bowl with a rubber spatula as needed.

INGREDIENTS

2½ pounds chicken thighs (about 8 thighs)

2 cups plus 1 teaspoon distilled white vinegar

2 cups finely chopped green onions (about 2 bunches)

2 jalapeños, seeded and minced

2 tablespoons soy sauce

2 tablespoons Kitchen Bouquet browning and seasoning sauce

4 tablespoons fresh lime juice

5 teaspoons ground allspice

2 bay leaves

6 garlic cloves, minced

1 tablespoon salt

2 teaspoons sugar

1½ teaspoons dried thyme, crumbled

1 teaspoon ground cinnamon

2 tablespoons vegetable oil

Jamaican Barbecue Sauce (recipe on page 103)

TOOLS

Measuring cups and spoons • cutting board • chef's knife • medium mixing bowl • rubber gloves • juicer (optional) • paper towels • 2 large resealable plastic food storage bags • food processor • rubber spatula • 13 x 9-inch baking dish • large nonstick skillet • tongs • oven mitts or pot holders

4. Reserve 2 tablespoons of the marinade for the Jamaican Barbecue Sauce (page 103).

5. Pour the remaining marinade inside the plastic bag to coat the chicken. Place the bag inside another resealable plastic food storage bag or in a shallow dish and refrigerate overnight.

> **CAUTION**
> Always handle jalapeño peppers with rubber gloves and be careful not to touch your eyes or skin.
> Please follow the directions for handling raw poultry on page 5 very carefully

6. Position rack in center of oven and preheat the oven to 375°F. Lightly grease a 13 by 9-inch baking dish and set aside.

7. Heat 1 tablespoon of the oil in a large nonstick skillet over medium-high heat.

8. Place half of the chicken thighs, skin side down, in the skillet and cook 2 minutes until skin is browned. Turn the chicken thighs using tongs and cook an additional 2 minutes.

9. Place the browned chicken thighs in the prepared baking dish.

10. Using oven mitts or pot holders, carefully wipe the hot skillet clean with paper towels.

11. Heat the remaining tablespoon of oil in the skillet and brown the remaining chicken thighs. Transfer the browned chicken to the baking dish.

12. Bake for 35 to 40 minutes, until chicken is cooked through.

13. Serve with Jamaican Barbecue Sauce.

DID YOU KNOW . . .

Jerk is not only a tasty flavoring, it's also a method of preserving fresh food without refrigeration, especially handy in hot climates like Jamaica.

JAMAICAN BARBECUE SAUCE

YIELD: About 2½ cups

INGREDIENTS

1¼ cups ketchup

⅓ cup soy sauce

2 tablespoons Pickapepper Sauce

2 tablespoons reserved jerk marinade (from previous page)

3 green onions, minced

3 garlic cloves, minced

3 tablespoons minced fresh ginger

⅓ cup dark brown sugar

⅓ cup distilled white vinegar

TOOLS

Measuring cups and spoons • cutting board • chef's knife • medium saucepan • wooden spoon • oven mitts or pot holders • food processor • rubber spatula

DIRECTIONS

CAUTION

1. In a medium saucepan, combine the ketchup, soy sauce, Pickapepper Sauce, reserved 2 tablespoons of jerk marinade, green onion, garlic, ginger, brown sugar, and vinegar.

2. Bring the sauce to a boil, stirring to dissolve the sugar.

3. Reduce the heat to a simmer and continue to cook another 12 minutes, until the sauce is slightly thickened.

4. Remove the sauce from the heat and cool to room temperature.

5. Place the sauce in a food processor and process until smooth, stopping to scrape down the sides of the bowl with a rubber spatula as needed.

6. Serve at room temperature with the Jamaican Jerked Chicken.

SWEDISH MEATBALLS

Boy, are these babies yummy, and kids love to help roll these little treats! The meatballs get a boost of flavor from the sauce they cook in, which has a secret ingredient that keeps everyone coming back for more. Now in Sweden meatballs are traditionally eaten with Swedish Cucumber Salad (page 62), boiled new potatoes, and lingonberry preserves—and the combination is simply awesome. But I love these with mashed potatoes, too.

HINT

These are great for parties and get-togethers because they taste even better if made a day or two in advance.

DID YOU KNOW . . .

These meatballs are an important part of a traditional Swedish buffet called a smorgasbord, literally meaning "open sandwich table." It's a great way to serve meals to a large crowd, especially during holidays.

INGREDIENTS

1½ cups finely chopped red onion

4½ tablespoons unsalted butter

¾ pound ground chuck

¾ pound ground pork

1¾ teaspoons salt

¾ teaspoon plus 1 pinch freshly ground black pepper

¼ teaspoon ground allspice

⅛ teaspoon ground nutmeg

1 cup plain dried bread crumbs

½ cup whole milk

1 cup heavy cream

1 large egg, lightly beaten

4 tablespoons all-purpose flour

2 (14-ounce) cans reduced-sodium beef broth

¼ cup red currant jelly

TOOLS

Measuring cups and spoons • cutting board • chef's knife • 2 medium skillets • medium mixing bowl • wooden spoon • small mixing bowl • large plate or baking dish • tongs or slotted spoon • Dutch oven or heavy large saucepan • can opener • whisk • oven mitts or pot holders

DIRECTIONS   CAUTION

1. In a medium skillet over medium-high heat, sauté 1 cup of the onion in 1½ tablespoons of the butter until soft and light golden brown, 4 to 6 minutes. Set aside to cool, then add the onion to a medium mixing bowl along with the ground chuck, ground pork, 1½ teaspoons of the salt, ½ teaspoon of the pepper, the allspice, and the nutmeg.

2. In a small mixing bowl, combine the bread crumbs with the milk and ¼ cup of the cream, and allow to sit until the bread crumbs are soft, about 5 minutes. Add the bread-crumb mixture and the beaten egg to the meat mixture and, using clean hands, mix well to thoroughly combine.

3. Using a tablespoon measure as a guide, scoop the meat mixture into meatball portions, about 1 heaping tablespoon each. Using lightly damp clean hands, roll the meatballs until they are smooth and round. Transfer to a large plate or baking dish while you form the remaining meatballs.

STEP 3

4. In a medium skillet, heat ½ tablespoon of the remaining butter until foamy. Add one-third of the meatballs and cook, turning frequently, until the meatballs are browned on all sides, 6 to 8 minutes total. Using tongs or a slotted spoon, transfer the cooked meatballs to a Dutch oven or heavy large saucepan and repeat with the remaining meatballs, adding another ½ tablespoon of butter to the skillet before each batch.

5. Add the remaining 1½ tablespoons of butter and the remaining ½ cup onion to the skillet and cook until the onion is soft, about 4 minutes. Add the flour and cook, stirring constantly, for 2 minutes. Whisk in the beef broth little by little and cook until the sauce is smooth and thick, about 4 minutes. Transfer the sauce to the Dutch oven or large saucepan and add the remaining ¼ teaspoon salt, a pinch of black pepper, the remaining heavy cream, and the currant jelly. Be careful when stirring not to break up the meatballs.

6. Bring the contents of the Dutch oven or large saucepan to a boil over medium-high heat, then reduce the heat so that the sauce simmers. Cook, uncovered, for 45 minutes to 1 hour, until the meatballs are very tender and the sauce is thick and flavorful.

PASTITSIO

(pah-STEET-see-oh)

This Greek layered casserole is a real crowd-pleaser. Layers of cooked pasta, meat sauce, and a creamy béchamel sauce combine to make something that is out of this world. With a loaf of hot, crusty bread and a green salad, you're in business. This casserole also can be assembled in advance and then baked just before serving, making it a great dish for parties.

INGREDIENTS

7 tablespoons unsalted butter

1½ pounds ground chuck

1 finely chopped yellow onion

1 teaspoon minced garlic

1¼ teaspoons salt

¼ teaspoon freshly ground black pepper

1 (14-ounce) can whole tomatoes, crushed, with juice

1 (14-ounce) can tomato sauce

1 bay leaf

½ teaspoon ground cinnamon

¼ cup all-purpose flour

3 cups whole milk

¼ teaspoon ground white pepper

¼ teaspoon freshly grated nutmeg

2 large eggs, lightly beaten

1 pound elbow macaroni

1½ cups finely grated pecorino Romano or Parmesan cheese

TOOLS

Measuring cups and spoons • cutting board • chef's knife• can opener • box grater • 2 medium saucepans • wooden spoon • large saucepan • whisk • colander • 13 x 9-inch casserole • spoon • oven mitts or pot holders

DIRECTIONS   CAUTION

1. In a medium saucepan over high heat, melt 2 tablespoons of the butter and add the ground chuck, chopped onion, garlic, ¾ teaspoon of the salt, and the black pepper. Cook, stirring, until meat has browned and the onion is translucent, about 6 minutes. Add the tomatoes, tomato sauce, bay leaf, and cinnamon, and bring to a low boil. Reduce the heat to a simmer and cook, uncovered, for 30 minutes, or until sauce is thick and flavorful.

TIP

This casserole reheats well. It's easier to cut if you let it sit before serving.

2. While the sauce is simmering, make the béchamel sauce. In a medium saucepan over medium-high heat, melt 4 tablespoons of the remaining butter. Whisk in the flour and cook for 2 minutes, whisking constantly. Do not allow the flour to brown. Little by little add the milk, whisking constantly. Cook the mixture until the sauce thickens and comes to a boil. Allow the sauce to boil gently for about 5 minutes, until very thick. Add the remaining ½ teaspoon of salt, the white pepper, nutmeg, and eggs, and whisk to combine. Set aside, covered, until ready to assemble the casserole.

3. Cook the macaroni in a large saucepan according to package directions and drain in a colander set in the sink.

4. Position rack in center of oven and preheat the oven to 350°F. Lightly grease a 13 by 9-inch casserole with the remaining tablespoon of butter. Transfer half of the cooked macaroni to the prepared casserole and top with half of the meat sauce. Repeat with the remaining macaroni and remaining meat sauce. Carefully spoon the béchamel over the meat sauce, using the back of a spoon to spread it so that it completely covers the sauce.

STEP 4

5. Spread the grated cheese evenly over the top of the casserole. Bake the casserole, uncovered, for 45 minutes to 1 hour, or until the cheese is golden brown on top.

6. Using oven mitts or pot holders, remove from the oven and let cool for at least 15 minutes before serving.

VEGETABLE CURRY

In India, where this dish hails from, cooks make their own curry powder, which is a blend of different spices. Some of the spices most often used are cumin, coriander, turmeric, cardamom, and ground hot chiles. Some blends have as many as twenty different spices! Here in America, we usually rely on store-bought curry powder for ease and convenience. I have added some garam masala to the recipe here, another blend that you should be able to find in grocery store spice aisles or gourmet markets. If you cannot find it, simply substitute an equal amount of regular curry powder.

INGREDIENTS

1/4 cup vegetable oil

1 medium yellow onion, chopped

2 tablespoons finely chopped fresh ginger

1 tablespoon minced garlic

2 tablespoons finely chopped jalapeño pepper

1 1/2 tablespoons curry powder

1 1/2 tablespoons garam masala or an additional 1 1/2 tablespoons curry powder

2 1/4 cups coconut milk

1 (28-ounce) can whole tomatoes, crushed, with juice

2 tablespoons sugar

1 1/2 teaspoons salt

1 medium Idaho potato, peeled and cut into 1-inch cubes

8 cups assorted vegetables, such as green beans, cauliflower florets, carrots, red and yellow bell peppers, zucchini, and eggplant, cut into bite-size pieces

1 (15-ounce) can chickpeas, drained and rinsed

Cooked basmati rice, for serving, prepared according to package intructions

TOOLS

Measuring cups and spoons • cutting board • chef's knife • rubber gloves • can opener • vegetable peeler • Dutch oven or large heavy saucepan with lid • wooden spoon • oven mitts or pot holders

DIRECTIONS   CAUTION

1. Heat the oil in a heavy Dutch oven or large heavy saucepan over high heat. Add the onion and cook until soft, about 4 minutes.

2. Add the ginger, garlic, jalapeño, curry powder, and garam masala and cook for 2 minutes, stirring, until fragrant.

> **CAUTION**
> Always handle jalapeño peppers with rubber gloves and be careful not to touch your eyes or skin.

3. Add the coconut milk, tomatoes, sugar, and salt, and bring to a boil. Reduce the heat to a simmer and cook for 10 minutes.

4. Add the potatoes and cook for 15 to 20 minutes, until the potatoes are just fork-tender.

5. Add the remaining vegetables and chickpeas. Stir well to combine, cover, and reduce the heat to medium-low. Cook, stirring only occasionally, until the vegetables are tender but not falling apart, 40 minutes to 1 hour.

6. Serve with hot cooked rice, preferably basmati if available.

DiD YOU KNOW . . .

Cooks in India make their own blend of curry powder and garam masala, and each region of India has its preference of flavors. That's why the unique taste in curry dishes varies so much from one region of India to another.

ARROZ CON POLLO

(ah-ROHS con POH-yoh)

 There are as many ways to make this classic Spanish dish as there are cooks, but this particular version comes to us by way of my close friend Jeanette. Originally from Ecuador, Jeanette is a fantastic cook and was kind enough to share her personal recipe for this wonderful dish. Since this makes a big batch, it is great for parties and family get-togethers.

DIRECTIONS   CAUTION

1. Wash the chicken quarters well under cold running water and place in a large (6-quart) saucepan. Add 6 cups of water.

   CAUTION Please follow the instructions for handling raw poultry on page 5 very carefully.

2. In a blender, combine the chopped onion, garlic, cumin, salt, black pepper, and ¼ cup water. Place the lid of the blender on tightly and blend on high speed until the mixture is liquefied and smooth, about 2 minutes.

3. Add this flavoring mixture to the pot with the chicken, and place the pot over high heat. Bring to a boil, skim any foam that rises to the surface, and reduce the heat to medium-low so that the liquid boils gently. Continue to cook, uncovered, for 45 minutes, until the chicken is very tender.

INGREDIENTS

1 medium chicken, quartered (about 3 pounds)

$\frac{1}{2}$ medium yellow onion, coarsely chopped

5 garlic cloves, smashed

1 tablespoon ground cumin

$2\frac{1}{4}$ teaspoons salt

$\frac{3}{4}$ teaspoon ground black pepper

$\frac{1}{4}$ cup water

1 tablespoon olive oil

3 pinches of saffron

2 cups long-grain white rice

6 tablespoons unsalted butter

1 medium yellow onion, thinly sliced lengthwise

$\frac{1}{2}$ red bell pepper, cut into $\frac{1}{4}$-inch-wide by 1-inch-long strips

$\frac{1}{2}$ yellow bell pepper, cut into $\frac{1}{4}$-inch-wide by 1-inch-long strips

$\frac{1}{2}$ green bell pepper, cut into $\frac{1}{4}$-inch-wide by 1-inch-long strips

$\frac{1}{4}$ cup stuffed green olives, sliced

$\frac{1}{4}$ cup capers, drained

2 tablespoons soy sauce

$\frac{1}{4}$ cup finely chopped green onions, for garnish

$\frac{1}{4}$ cup finely chopped fresh cilantro, for garnish

TOOLS

Measuring cups and spoons • cutting board • chef's knife • large (6-quart) saucepan with lid • blender • tongs • large plate or baking sheet • fine-mesh sieve • medium mixing bowl • wooden spoon • large nonstick skillet • oven mitts or pot holders

---

DID YOU KNOW . . .

Saffron is the most expensive spice in the world and is actually the dried stigma of the crocus flower.

4. Remove the chicken quarters from the cooking liquid with tongs, place on a large plate or baking sheet, and set aside to cool. Strain the cooking liquid through a fine-mesh sieve into a medium mixing bowl and discard the solids. Return 4 cups of the cooking liquid to the saucepan and reserve any remaining cooking liquid on the side.

5. When the chicken has cooled enough to handle, discard the skin and bones and tear the meat into bite-size pieces. Set aside. Wash your hands well before proceeding.

STEP 5

6. Add the olive oil and saffron to the 4 cups of cooking liquid in the saucepan and bring to a boil over high heat. Add the rice and stir to combine. When the liquid returns to a boil, stir the rice once more, then cover the saucepan, and reduce the heat to medium-low. Cook the rice, undisturbed, for 20 minutes, until it is tender and has absorbed the cooking liquid. Set aside.

7. While the rice is cooking, heat a large nonstick skillet over medium-high heat and add the butter. When the butter has melted, add the sliced onion, bell peppers, olives, and capers, and cook for 2 minutes, until the vegetables are just beginning to soften. Add the reserved chicken and the soy sauce, and continue to cook over medium-high heat, stirring occasionally, until the vegetables are soft and the flavors have blended, about 15 minutes. If the mixture begins to stick before the vegetables are soft, add a bit of the reserved cooking liquid to the pan and stir to release any bits stuck to the bottom. Set aside.

8. When the rice is cooked, add the chicken mixture to the pot with the rice and stir gently to combine. Cover the pot and allow the mixture to sit for 15 to 20 minutes to allow flavors to blend. Garnish with the chopped green onions and cilantro and serve.

KOREAN-STYLE PORK WRAPS WITH CHILI SAUCE

These pork wraps are so much fun to eat—they are like Korean tacos with lettuce instead of taco shells! You can get creative with toppings, too! I like to add chopped cucumbers and thinly sliced carrots on top of my pork wraps. Watch out if you don't like things spicy, but I think the hot chili sauce is out of this world! If you prefer, start out slowly, using 1 tablespoon of chili sauce. However, I like it full strength.

INGREDIENTS

1½ pounds pork tenderloin, trimmed

¼ cup soy sauce

1 tablespoon sugar

4 teaspoons toasted sesame oil

½ cup chopped green onions

1 tablespoon minced garlic

1 tablespoon minced fresh ginger

2 tablespoons Sriracha hot chili sauce

4 teaspoons honey

1 tablespoon vegetable oil

2 tablespoons sesame seeds, toasted

1½ cups cooked jasmine rice

1 head Boston, bibb, or butter lettuce, leaves separated, washed, and patted dry

TOOLS

Measuring cups and spoons • cutting board • chef's knife • vegetable peeler (optional) • plastic wrap • medium mixing bowl • whisk • small mixing bowl • large skillet • slotted spoon • tongs or wooden spoon • oven mitts or pot holders

DIRECTIONS CAUTION

1. Wrap the pork tenderloin in several sheets of plastic wrap and place in the freezer for 40 minutes. (This is to make it easier to thinly slice, so make sure it doesn't freeze completely.)

> **CAUTION**
> Please follow the directions for cooking pork on page 26 very carefully.

2. In a medium mixing bowl, combine the soy sauce, sugar, 2 teaspoons of the sesame oil, green onion, garlic, and ginger. Whisk together until the sugar dissolves.

3. Take the pork out of the freezer and unwrap on a clean cutting board. Slice the pork into thin strips, about ¼ inch thick, ¼ inch wide, and 2½ inches long. Place the pork strips in the soy marinade, cover, and refrigerate for 1 hour.

STEP 3

4. In a small mixing bowl, combine the Sriracha hot chili sauce, the honey, and the remaining 2 teaspoons of sesame oil. Stir to combine. Set aside.

5. When the pork has marinated, take the bowl out of the refrigerator and let it sit at room temperature for 15 minutes.

6. Heat the vegetable oil in a large skillet over high heat.

7. Using a slotted spoon, remove the pork from the marinade and carefully place in the skillet. (Be careful that the drippings don't splatter out of the pan.)

8. Cook the pork, stirring constantly with tongs or a wooden spoon, 4 to 5 minutes, until the pork is cooked through.

9. Remove from the heat and stir in the sesame seeds.

10. To serve, spoon several tablespoons of rice into the center of a lettuce leaf, taco-style. Top with a few pork strips and drizzle with a few drops of the chili mixture. Roll up and eat!

STEP 10

CHICKEN CORDON BLEU

(kor-dohn BLUH)

The name of this dish translates from the French as "blue ribbon," and refers to a prestigious award once given to chefs for cooking excellence. It's the perfect name for this classic French dish, which has become an international favorite! A chicken breast is stuffed with Swiss cheese and ham and then breaded and pan-fried for an out-of-this-world combination. Try eating yours over pasta or with a simple rice pilaf.

114

YIELD: 4 servings

INGREDIENTS

4 (4- to 5-ounce) boneless, skinless chicken breast halves

½ teaspoon salt

½ teaspoon ground black pepper

8 very-thin slices baked ham

8 slices Swiss cheese (about 8 ounces)

1 cup all-purpose flour

2 large eggs

2 tablespoons whole milk

1 cup Italian-style bread crumbs

1 teaspoon Emeril's Original Essence

¼ cup olive oil

2 tablespoons unsalted butter

TOOLS

Measuring cups and spoons • cutting board • wax paper or plastic wrap • meat mallet or rolling pin • 3 medium mixing bowls • whisk • large plate • large nonstick skillet • spatula or tongs • paper towel–lined plate • oven mitts or pot holders

---

DIRECTIONS CAUTION

1. On a clean cutting board, spread out 1 sheet of wax paper or plastic wrap. Place 1 chicken breast on the wax paper and top with a second sheet.

   CAUTION Please follow the directions for handling raw poultry on page 5 very carefully.

2. Using a meat mallet or rolling pin, pound the chicken breast until it is evenly flattened to about ¼ inch thick. Repeat with remaining chicken breast halves. (You may need new sheets of wax paper or plastic wrap for each breast.)

STEP 2

3. Spread the chicken breasts out and sprinkle ⅛ teaspoon of salt and pepper on each. Layer 2 slices of ham and 2 slices of Swiss cheese on each. Fold the chicken breasts in half and press to flatten and seal the edges, making sure the ham and cheese are tucked securely inside each chicken breast.

STEP 3

4. Place the flour in a medium mixing bowl. In a second medium mixing bowl, whisk together the eggs and milk. Mix together the bread crumbs and Essence in a third medium mixing bowl.

5. Carefully dip each folded chicken breast one at a time into the flour mixture, dusting off the excess flour. Then dip the chicken into the egg mixture, then coat well with the bread crumb mixture, patting to make sure the bread crumbs stick well to the chicken. Place the breaded chicken on a large plate, cover, and refrigerate for 20 minutes.

STEP 5

6. In a large nonstick skillet, heat the olive oil over medium heat.

7. When the oil gets very hot, but not smoking, carefully place the chicken breasts into the skillet with 1 tablespoon of the butter, being careful not to overcrowd the pan. Cook until golden brown, 4 to 5 minutes. Using a spatula or tongs, carefully turn the chicken breasts and add the remaining tablespoon of butter. Cook for an additional 4 to 5 minutes, until the chicken is browned and cooked through.

8. Remove the chicken from the pan and place on a paper towel–lined plate to drain.

9. Serve immediately, and be careful when cutting into the chicken, as the hot cheese will ooze out.

TOURTIÈRE QUÉBECOISE

(TOUR-tee-air KEH-behk-wahz)

Don't let the fancy French name fool you—this is Canadian home cooking at its best. In Quebec province, where a good portion of Canadians still speak French, this traditional meat pie is standard fare in many homes. It makes a hearty dinner when served with a vegetable or a simple green salad.

INGREDIENTS

¼ pound bacon, cut into ½-inch pieces

1½ pounds lean ground pork

1½ teaspoons Emeril's Original Essence

¼ teaspoon salt

¼ teaspoon ground black pepper

¼ teaspoon ground cinnamon

⅛ teaspoon ground cloves

1½ cups chopped yellow onion

⅓ cup chopped celery

2 tablespoons finely chopped garlic

1 tablespoon finely chopped fresh savory or 1 teaspoon dried savory

2 tablespoons all-purpose flour

2 cups reduced-sodium chicken broth

1 cup water

1 bay leaf

2 tablespoons finely chopped fresh parsley

Pastry for a double-crust savory pie (recipe on page 119) or store-bought pastry for a double-crust pie

1 large egg yolk, beaten with 1 tablespoon milk

TOOLS

Measuring cups and spoons • cutting board • chef's knife • large heavy saucepan • can opener (optional) • wooden spoon • medium mixing bowl • rolling pin • 9- or 9½-inch deep-dish pie pan • spoon • fork • paring knife • pastry brush • oven mitts or pot holders

DIRECTIONS

CAUTION

CAUTION Please follow the directions for handling meat on page 5 very carefully.

1. In a large heavy saucepan over medium-high heat, cook the bacon until it is crisp and has released almost all of its fat, about 6 minutes. This is called rendering. Add the pork, Essence, salt, pepper, cinnamon, and cloves and cook, stirring to break up any lumps, until the meat is well browned, about 6 minutes. Add the onion and celery and cook until vegetables are soft, about 4 minutes. Add the garlic and cook for 1 minute. Add the savory and flour and cook, stirring, for 2 minutes.

2. Add the chicken broth, water, and bay leaf and cook, stirring occasionally, for about 30 minutes, until almost all of the liquid has evaporated and the meat is tender and flavorful. Stir in the parsley. Taste and adjust the seasoning, if necessary. Remove the bay leaf, which is bitter and non-edible. Set the filling aside to cool to room temperature, then transfer to a medium mixing bowl and refrigerate, covered, until thoroughly chilled, about 2 hours or up to overnight.

3. Prepare the piecrust according to the recipe on page 119. On a lightly floured surface, use a rolling pin to roll out one disk of the dough to a thickness of ⅛ inch. Gently fold the pastry circle in half, then in half again so that you can lift it without tearing it. Then unfold it into a 9- or 9½- by 2-inch deep-dish pie pan. Trim the edges so that they are even and extend about ½ inch beyond the edge of the pie pan.

STEP 3

4. Spoon the chilled meat mixture into the piecrust. Lightly brush the edges of the pastry with some of the beaten egg yolk.

5. Again on a lightly floured work surface, roll out the remaining pastry disk to a thickness of ⅛ inch. Fold the pastry as before, then transfer it to the top of the pie and gently unfold it. Trim the edges so that they match up with the bottom crust and press to seal (page 22).

STEP 5

(continued)

6. Using your fingers, carefully tuck any excess pastry into the side of the pie pan and, using your fingers or a fork, press or crimp the pastry in regular intervals to form a decorative edge. Using a sharp paring knife, cut several small steam vents in the top of the pastry so that steam may escape while the pie is cooking. Refrigerate the pie for at least 15 minutes before baking.

STEP 6

7. Position rack on lowest rung of oven and preheat the oven to 425°F.

8. Using a pastry brush, lightly brush the top of the pie with some of the remaining beaten egg yolk mixture. Bake the pie for 20 minutes, then reduce the heat to 350°F, and continue to bake the pie until the crust is golden brown, another 35 to 40 minutes.

BASIC PIECRUST FOR A SAVORY PIE

YIELD: Two 9- or 10-inch single piecrusts, or enough dough for 1 double-crust pie

INGREDIENTS

3 cups plus 4 tablespoons all-purpose flour

1 teaspoon salt

16 tablespoons (2 sticks) cold unsalted butter, cut into ½-inch pieces

4 tablespoons cold solid vegetable shortening

6 tablespoons ice water

TOOLS

Measuring cups and spoons • sifter • large mixing bowl • plastic wrap

DIRECTIONS   CAUTION

STEP 2

1. Sift the flour and salt into a large mixing bowl.

2. Using your fingertips, work the butter and shortening into the flour until the mixture resembles small peas. Work the ice water into the mixture with your fingers until the dough just comes together; be careful not to overmix.

3. Form the dough into two disks, making one disk slightly larger than the other. Wrap the disks tightly in plastic wrap and refrigerate for at least 30 minutes and up to overnight before rolling out (page 22). The larger portion of dough should be used for the bottom crust of the pie.

Note: For a single-crust pie, simply divide all ingredients in half. When the dough comes together, form it into one disk. Refrigerate as instructed.

CHICKEN PICCATA

(pih-KAH-tuh)

"Piccata" refers to a classic Italian preparation in which either veal or chicken is pounded thin and then breaded and pan-fried with a lemon, butter, and parsley sauce. I like to use chicken when I make piccata, but feel free to use veal if you like.

DiD YOU KNOW . . .

Capers are actually flower buds preserved in salt or pickled. They are believed to have originated in western or central Asia, but they have become a key ingredient in the cuisine of Mediterranean countries.

120

INGREDIENTS

4 boneless, skinless chicken breast halves

½ cup all-purpose flour

1¾ teaspoons salt

½ teaspoon freshly ground black pepper

3 tablespoons vegetable oil

6 tablespoons unsalted butter

¼ cup fresh lemon juice

½ cup reduced-sodium chicken broth

1 garlic clove, minced

2 tablespoons drained capers

1 tablespoon chopped fresh parsley

TOOLS

Measuring cups and spoons • cutting board • chef's knife • juicer (optional) • can opener (optional) • wax paper or plastic wrap • meat mallet or rolling pin • shallow bowl • large skillet • tongs • wooden spoon • oven mitts or pot holders

DIRECTIONS   CAUTION

1. On a clean cutting board, spread out 1 sheet of wax paper or plastic wrap. Place 1 chicken breast on the wax paper and top with a second sheet.

   CAUTION Please follow the directions for handling raw poultry on page 5 very carefully.

2. Using a meat mallet or rolling pin, pound the chicken breast until it is evenly flattened to about ⅛ inch thick. Repeat with the remaining chicken breast halves. (You may need new sheets of wax paper or plastic wrap for each breast.) Set aside.

STEP 2

3. In a shallow bowl, combine the flour, 1½ teaspoons of the salt, and the pepper, and stir to combine.

4. Quickly dredge the pounded chicken in the flour mixture, shaking to remove any excess flour.

STEP 4

5. Place 1½ tablespoons of the oil in a large skillet over medium-high heat. When the oil gets very hot, but not smoking, add 1 tablespoon of the butter and, working quickly, add half of the chicken and cook for 1 minute, until golden.

6. Using tongs, turn the chicken and cook until golden and cooked through, about 1½ minutes. Remove the chicken from the skillet and cover to keep warm.

7. Repeat with the remaining 1½ tablespoons of oil, 1 tablespoon of butter, and pounded chicken, cooking as above. Remove the chicken from the skillet and cover to keep warm.

8. Add the lemon juice to the skillet, scraping with a wooden spoon to remove any browned bits from the bottom of the pan. When the juice has reduced by half, about 1 minute, add the chicken broth, garlic, and capers, and cook for 5 minutes, until slightly thickened. Add the remaining ¼ teaspoon of salt, remaining 4 tablespoons of butter, and parsley. Cook, stirring, until heated through and the sauce has thickened, about 1 minute. Do not allow sauce to boil.

9. Remove from the heat and pour the sauce over the reserved chicken. Serve immediately.

PUERTO RICAN ROAST PORK

This Puerto Rican classic roast pork is super easy and delicious and feeds a crowd! Just make sure to marinate the meat overnight, as this really helps the flavors of the garlic and oregano seep into the meat. There are lots of ways to serve this: Make a whole meal by serving it alongside the Portuguese Rice (page 144) and Refried Beans (page 146) or with the African-Inspired Sweet Potato Puree (page 142), or add any leftovers to burritos or tacos. The cooking time might seem lengthy but trust me, this results in a moist, flavorful roast that is falling-apart good.

DID YOU KNOW . . .

The island of Puerto Rico was originally inhabited by the Tainos and then later by the Spanish, British, French, Dutch, and the African slaves they brought with them. These influences are easily seen in Puerto Rican cuisine, which is called "cocina criolla."

INGREDIENTS

1 (6- to 8-pound) bone-in pork shoulder roast, such as Boston butt or picnic roast

3 tablespoons olive oil

3 tablespoons distilled white vinegar

2 tablespoons salt

2 tablespoons minced garlic

2 teaspoons crushed dried oregano

$\frac{1}{2}$ teaspoon black pepper

TOOLS

Measuring cups and spoons • cutting board • chef's knife • paring knife • small mixing bowl • large nonreactive bowl • plastic wrap • roasting pan • aluminum foil • meat baster • platter or baking sheet • two forks • large spoon • oven mitts or pot holders

DIRECTIONS

CAUTION

1. Wash the pork shoulder roast under cool running water and pat dry. With a sharp paring knife, make 1-inch-deep incisions all over the roast. If the roast still has a thick layer of fat and skin on one side, use a sharp slicing knife to make long scores through the fat and into the meaty part of the roast in several places. The scores should penetrate the meat by at least $\frac{1}{2}$ inch. This will be the top of your roast. (If your roast does not have any skin or exterior fat, scoring is not necessary.) Wash hands well before continuing.

> **CAUTION** Please follow the directions for handling raw meat on page 5 carefully.

STEP 1

2. Add all the remaining ingredients to a small mixing bowl and stir well to combine. Using clean hands, spread this mixture all over the roast, rubbing it in very well. Any mixture that is left may be spooned into the scores on the top of the roast, if applicable. Wash hands well.

3. Transfer the seasoned roast to a large nonreactive bowl and cover with plastic wrap. Refrigerate overnight.

4. Remove the roast from the refrigerator and allow it to come to room temperature, from 30 minutes to 1 hour, before proceeding.

5. Position rack in center of oven and preheat the oven to 350°F. Line a roasting pan with aluminum foil. Transfer the roast to the prepared pan and pour any accumulated juices over it. Cover with aluminum foil and bake, undisturbed, for 4 hours. Using oven mitts or pot holders, remove the foil from the roast and continue to bake, basting occasionally with the drippings from the bottom of the pan, for 2 more hours, until the roast is golden brown and crispy on the outside and the flesh is fork-tender.

6. Using oven mitts or pot holders, remove roast from the oven. Carefully transfer the roast to a platter or baking sheet and let rest for 20 minutes. Use two forks to pull the meat away from the bone into pieces. The meat should pull apart easily. Discard the bone and any excess fat.

7. Using a large spoon, skim the fat from the drippings in the bottom of the roasting pan and discard. Serve the meat with any remaining pan juices. If the juices have browned and caramelized on the pan bottom, try adding a bit of warm water and stirring to reconstitute the drippings.

IRISH SALMON PIE

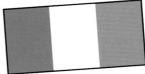

 This Irish pie combines three of the quintessential flavors of the Emerald Isle—salmon, potatoes, and fresh leeks—for one super dinner. Serve it with a green salad for a meal that is sure to make Irish eyes smile!

DIRECTIONS

CAUTION 👁 🔪 🔥 🧤 ✋

1. Prepare the pastry as instructed on page 119 and chill in the refrigerator while you prepare the filling.

2. In a small pot, cover the potatoes with water by 1 inch. Bring to a boil and cook until the potatoes are just fork-tender, about 5 minutes. Drain potatoes in a colander set in the sink and refresh under cold running water, being careful not to break the pieces.

3. Season the salmon lightly on both sides with ¼ teaspoon of the salt and ¼ teaspoon of the white pepper.

4. In a medium skillet, bring the chicken broth to a simmer. Add the salmon and cook until just cooked through, about 8 minutes.

INGREDIENTS

Pastry for a double-crust savory pie
(page 119) or store-bought
pastry for double-crust savory pie

¾ pound Idaho potato, peeled and
cut into ¼-inch slices

1 pound skinless salmon fillets

¾ teaspoon salt

½ teaspoon ground white pepper

2 cups reduced-sodium chicken broth

¼ pound thickly cut bacon, cut
into 1-inch pieces

1 cup sliced leeks, whites only,
rinsed well (page 14)

2 teaspoons minced garlic

1 tablespoon finely chopped fresh
parsley

2 large eggs

1 large egg yolk

½ cup plus 1 tablespoon heavy
cream

Melted unsalted butter, for serving

Lemon wedges, for serving

TOOLS

Measuring cups and spoons •
cutting board • chef's knife •
vegetable peeler • small pot •
colander • medium skillet • can
opener (optional) • skimmer or
slotted spoon • large mixing bowl
• large skillet • paper towels •
wooden spoon • small mixing bowl
• fork or whisk • rolling pin •
10-inch pie pan • spoon • paring
knife or kitchen shears • fork
(optional) • pastry brush • oven
mitts or pot holders • wire rack

This is called poaching. Remove from the heat and, using a skimmer or slotted spoon, transfer the salmon to a large mixing bowl to cool. When cool enough to handle, gently break salmon into bite-size pieces.

5. In a large skillet over medium-high heat, cook the bacon until it is crisp and has released almost all of its fat, about 6 minutes. This is called rendering. Remove the bacon with a slotted spoon and transfer to paper towels to drain. Drain off all but 2 tablespoons of the fat from the skillet. Add the leeks and cook, stirring occasionally, until soft, about 6 minutes. Add the garlic and cook, stirring, for 1 minute. Remove from the heat, add the parsley, and set aside to cool.

6. Add the leek mixture to the salmon and mix gently, being careful not to break up the fish pieces.

7. In a small mixing bowl, with a fork or whisk, beat together the eggs, egg yolk, ½ cup of the cream, the remaining salt, and the remaining white pepper.

8. Position rack in bottom third of oven and preheat the oven to 375°F.

9. On a lightly floured surface, roll out the larger piece of dough into a round, about 12 inches in diameter and about ⅛ inch thick. Transfer to a 10-inch pie pan. Lay the bacon pieces across the bottom, and top with the potato slices. Spoon the salmon mixture over the potatoes and top with the cream mixture. Roll out the remaining dough and transfer to the top of the pie. Using a small sharp knife or kitchen shears, cut away the excess dough and crimp the edges of the crusts with your fingers or a fork to seal completely. Cut several thin vents in the crust with the knife and, with a pastry brush, paint the top crust with the remaining tablespoon of cream.

STEP 9

10. Bake the pie until golden brown, 1 hour to 1 hour and 15 minutes. Using oven mitts or pot holders, remove from the oven and cool on a wire rack for 15 minutes before serving.

STEP 9

11. To serve, cut the pie into 6 to 8 slices and drizzle each slice with some of the melted butter. Serve with a lemon wedge for squeezing.

BBQ RIBS

Americans really love their barbecue, and ribs are a huge favorite. These baby back ribs are super easy to prepare, and because they're cooked long and slow in the oven, they are fall-from-the-bone tender. While there are lots of really good bottled barbecue sauces on the market, nothing is better than homemade, and these ribs won't be quite the same without it.

CAUTION An adult should always remove the pan with the water from the oven. It's best to wait until the oven has cooled to remove it, otherwise both the pan and the water will be very hot and could easily spill. But go ahead and remove the pan with the ribs while they're hot!

DIRECTIONS   CAUTION

1. Fill a small baking pan two-thirds full with cold water and place on the lowest rung in the oven. This helps to keep the ribs moist during the lengthy cooking time.

2. Position a second rack in the middle of the oven. Preheat the oven to 275°F. Line a large baking sheet with aluminum foil.

DID YOU KNOW . . .
Barbecuing originated in the New World with the Native Americans, who taught the colonists how to cook meats and fish this way. In colonial times, a barbecue meant a big, festive community gathering, and it is said that George Washington hosted the first barbecue in 1769.

126

INGREDIENTS

Ribs:

2 racks baby back pork ribs, about 1½ pounds each, trimmed

1 teaspoon salt

½ teaspoon black pepper

2 tablespoons light brown sugar

¼ teaspoon cayenne

BBQ sauce:

4 tablespoons unsalted butter

1½ cups finely chopped yellow onion

6 garlic cloves, finely chopped

2¼ teaspoons sweet paprika

2 teaspoons Emeril's Bayou Blast or other Creole seasoning

2 teaspoons dry mustard

1¼ teaspoons salt

½ teaspoon crushed red pepper

½ teaspoon black pepper

¼ teaspoon cayenne

1 (6-ounce) can tomato paste

1½ cups water

¾ cup cider vinegar

¾ cup plus 2 tablespoons dark brown sugar

TOOLS

Measuring cups and spoons • cutting board • chef's knife • can opener • small baking pan • large baking sheet • aluminum foil • small mixing bowl • medium nonreactive saucepan • wooden spoon • blender • small nonreactive bowl • oven mitts or pot holders • basting brush • tongs • sharp knife

3. To prepare the ribs, in a small mixing bowl combine the salt, black pepper, light brown sugar, and cayenne, and toss to combine. Divide the spice mixture equally between the two racks of ribs and, with clean hands, rub into the meat well on both sides.

4. Place the ribs on the foil-lined baking sheet and bake for 2 hours, uncovered.

5. While the ribs are baking, make the BBQ sauce: In a medium nonreactive saucepan over medium-high heat, add the butter and, when melted, add the onion and cook until it is very soft, about 4 minutes. Add the garlic, paprika, Bayou Blast or other Creole seasoning, dry mustard, salt, crushed red pepper, black pepper, and cayenne, and cook for 2 minutes. Add the tomato paste and cook, stirring frequently, for 2 minutes, until the tomato paste begins to brown. Add the water, cider vinegar, and dark brown sugar and stir to combine. Reduce the heat to low and cook until the sauce has thickened and the flavors have come together, about 15 minutes. Set aside to cool.

6. When cooled, transfer the sauce to a blender. Puree until very smooth, 1 to 2 minutes, then transfer the sauce to a small nonreactive bowl and set aside.

7. When the ribs have baked for 2 hours, use oven mitts or pot holders to remove the baking sheet from the oven. Using a basting brush and tongs to turn the ribs, lightly coat both sides of both racks of ribs with some of the BBQ sauce. Return the ribs to the oven and bake for 15 minutes.

8. Using oven mitts or pot holders, remove the baking sheet from the oven and, using tongs, carefully turn the ribs. Return the ribs to the oven and bake for 15 minutes longer. Remove the ribs and let cool slightly.

9. Using a sharp knife, cut the racks of ribs into individual ribs for serving. Serve immediately, with the extra BBQ sauce at the table.

STEP **9**

127

SHRIMP SCAMPI

(SKAM-pee)

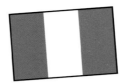

An Italian-American favorite, this popular dish is served in restaurants all over America because everybody just loves it. I hope you enjoy this family-friendly version with lots of tangy lemon juice and garlic. Serve the shrimp over your favorite pasta or rice!

INGREDIENTS

1½ pounds small shrimp, peeled and deveined (page 17)

¾ teaspoon salt

¼ teaspoon ground black pepper

2 tablespoons olive oil

3½ tablespoons fresh lemon juice

1 tablespoon minced garlic

½ cup reduced-sodium chicken broth

1 tablespoon sliced green onion

3 tablespoons unsalted butter

1 tablespoon chopped fresh parsley

1 pound bucatini pasta or other favorite pasta, cooked according to package instructions

TOOLS

Measuring cups and spoons • cutting board • chef's knife • juicer (optional) • can opener (optional) • medium mixing bowl • large skillet • wooden spoon • oven mitts or pot holders

DIRECTIONS   CAUTION

1. In a medium mixing bowl, season the shrimp with ½ teaspoon of the salt and the pepper. Toss to coat.

2. Heat the olive oil in a large skillet over medium-high heat. Add the shrimp and cook, stirring occasionally, for 2 to 3 minutes, until pink.

3. Add the lemon juice, garlic, chicken broth, green onion, and the remaining ¼ teaspoon of salt to the skillet. Bring to a boil and cook until slightly reduced, 2 to 3 minutes.

4. Remove the pan from the heat and stir in the butter and chopped parsley.

5. Toss with the cooked pasta and serve hot.

A GUIDE
TO SIDES

MOROCCAN COUSCOUS

(KOOS-koos)

Couscous is eaten all over North Africa and is particularly associated with Moroccan cooking, where it is usually served for lunch on Fridays. Though traditionally a main course or dessert, the quick cooking time makes this a wonderful side dish for any number of entrées. Feel free to kick yours up by adding your favorite dried fruits, nuts, citrus zest, or small vegetables or garbanzo beans.

DiD YOU KNOW . . .

Couscous is a classic Berber dish. The Berbers are the indigenous people of Morocco.

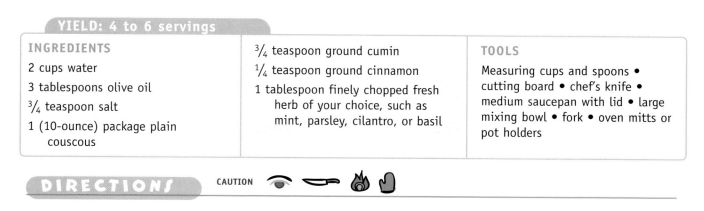

INGREDIENTS

2 cups water

3 tablespoons olive oil

¾ teaspoon salt

1 (10-ounce) package plain couscous

¾ teaspoon ground cumin

¼ teaspoon ground cinnamon

1 tablespoon finely chopped fresh herb of your choice, such as mint, parsley, cilantro, or basil

TOOLS

Measuring cups and spoons • cutting board • chef's knife • medium saucepan with lid • large mixing bowl • fork • oven mitts or pot holders

DIRECTIONS

CAUTION

1. In a medium saucepan, bring the water, 1 tablespoon of the olive oil, and ½ teaspoon of the salt to a boil.

2. When the water begins to boil, remove the pan from the heat, stir in the couscous, and cover the saucepan. Allow the couscous to stand for 5 minutes, without lifting the lid.

3. Pour the couscous into a large mixing bowl and toss lightly with a fork to break up any lumps.

4. Drizzle the couscous with the remaining 2 tablespoons of olive oil, tossing to coat well.

5. Add the remaining ¼ teaspoon salt, cumin, cinnamon, and herb of your choice. Gently toss to combine, using a fork to stir in the seasonings.

GREEN BEAN STIR-FRY

This super-quick Chinese veggie side dish will go great with the Shrimp Teriyaki on page 98. These green beans are so good, even a picky eater might change his or her mind after trying one. Make sure you have all your ingredients ready to go before you begin, because it really doesn't take long to make these beans, thanks to this Asian cooking technique!

INGREDIENTS

1 pound fresh green beans, washed and ends trimmed

1 tablespoon toasted sesame oil

1 tablespoon minced garlic

1½ teaspoons minced fresh ginger

2 tablespoons sliced green onions (white part only)

½ cup julienned red bell pepper (about ½ medium pepper)

1½ tablespoons soy sauce

1 teaspoon oyster sauce

2 teaspoons teriyaki sauce, store-bought or homemade (page 99)

¼ teaspoon salt

TOOLS

Measuring cups and spoons • cutting board • chef's knife • large stockpot • medium mixing bowl • tongs or slotted spoon • colander • clean, dry kitchen towels or paper towels • large nonstick skillet • wooden spoon • oven mitts or pot holders

DIRECTIONS   CAUTION

1. Fill a large stockpot with salted water and bring to a boil over high heat.

2. Prepare a medium mixing bowl by filling it with ice water.

3. Cook green beans in boiling water for 2½ to 3 minutes, until crisp-tender.

4. Using tongs or a slotted spoon, remove the green beans from the boiling water and place immediately into the bowl of ice water, to stop the cooking process.

5. When beans are cooled, drain and place on clean, dry kitchen towels or paper towels. Pat the beans dry, making sure there is no water on the beans before continuing.

6. Heat the sesame oil in a large nonstick skillet over medium-high heat. Carefully add the green beans and cook, stirring constantly, for 1 to 2 minutes.

7. Add the garlic, ginger, and green onions, and cook, stirring, an additional 30 seconds to 1 minute, being careful not to burn the garlic.

8. Stir in the red bell pepper, soy sauce, oyster sauce, teriyaki sauce, and salt. Stir to heat through, about 1 to 2 minutes longer. Serve immediately.

MEXICAN BROILED CORN

This is not your average corn on the cob! In Mexico, they like to shake things up by adding the flavors of lime juice, chiles, cheese, and even sour cream or mayonnaise, and the corn is served from street carts as midday snacks. I like to use queso fresco, a white, crumbly type of cheese from Mexico, but if you can't find this cheese, Parmesan works great, too. Once you try this dish, you may never go back to plain corn on the cob again!

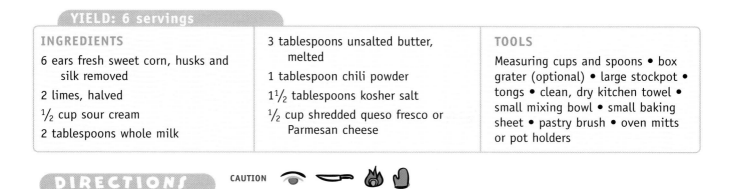

INGREDIENTS

6 ears fresh sweet corn, husks and silk removed

2 limes, halved

½ cup sour cream

2 tablespoons whole milk

3 tablespoons unsalted butter, melted

1 tablespoon chili powder

1½ tablespoons kosher salt

½ cup shredded queso fresco or Parmesan cheese

TOOLS

Measuring cups and spoons • box grater (optional) • large stockpot • tongs • clean, dry kitchen towel • small mixing bowl • small baking sheet • pastry brush • oven mitts or pot holders

DIRECTIONS

CAUTION

1. Fill a large stockpot with water and bring to a boil over high heat.

> **CAUTION**
> Please have an adult help you to use your broiler.

2. Place the corn and 2 lime halves into the boiling water and boil for 6 to 8 minutes, until the corn is tender. Use tongs to remove the corn from the water and place on a clean, dry kitchen towel to remove excess water.

3. In a small mixing bowl, combine the sour cream and milk and set aside.

4. Place the corn on a small baking sheet and brush with melted butter.

5. Arrange the oven rack 8 inches from the broiler unit and adjust the oven settings to broil.

6. Using oven mitts or pot holders, place the baking sheet in the oven and broil for 8 to 10 minutes, taking the corn out and using a pastry brush to baste with melted butter every 2 to 3 minutes. Watch the corn carefully while it is in the oven to prevent excessive browning. The corn should be golden brown when ready.

7. Using oven mitts or pot holders, remove the baking sheet from the oven and squeeze the remaining lime halves over the warm corn.

8. Generously brush the corn with the sour cream mixture and sprinkle with chili powder, salt, and shredded cheese. Serve warm.

STEAMED BROCCOLI WITH HOLLANDAISE (HOL-uhn-dayz)

Hollandaise is a classic French sauce which everyone loves but is afraid to make at home. We make it easily in a blender, and once you try it I bet you'll be whipping up batches of this sauce for all sorts of dishes. It works wonders with many of your favorite vegetables, or try it over poached eggs and English muffins for a super-easy brunch treat!

INGREDIENTS

1 bunch broccoli, stems trimmed to 4-inch florets, florets cut into halves or quarters lengthwise

3 egg yolks, at room temperature

1½ tablespoons fresh lemon juice, at room temperature

¼ teaspoon plus 1 pinch of salt

Pinch of cayenne

½ cup unsalted butter, cut into pieces

TOOLS

Measuring cups and spoons • cutting board • chef's knife •

medium saucepan with steamer insert and lid • tongs • serving bowl or platter • aluminum foil or plastic wrap • blender • small saucepan • small nonreactive serving bowl • spoon • oven mitts or pot holders

DIRECTIONS

CAUTION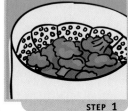

1. Add 2 inches of water to a medium saucepan. Place a steamer insert in the saucepan and bring the water to a boil. Place the broccoli inside the steamer and cover with a lid.

STEP 1

2. Steam the broccoli until crisp-tender, about 6 minutes. Using tongs, transfer the broccoli to a serving bowl or platter and lightly cover with aluminum foil or plastic wrap while you make the hollandaise.

3. Combine the egg yolks, lemon juice, salt, and cayenne in a blender and blend on high speed for 20 seconds, until the mixture is completely smooth.

4. Place the butter in a small saucepan and melt over medium heat until bubbly. Do not allow to brown.

5. With the blender running at high speed, and working very carefully, add the melted butter in a thin, steady stream through the pour hole in the top of blender. If this is too difficult, ask an adult to help. It is important that the butter is added very slowly at first; then, after you see that the sauce is beginning to thicken, you can add the butter a bit more quickly. It should take about 30 seconds to add all of the butter. Then turn off the blender immediately.

STEP 5

6. Transfer the hollandaise to a small nonreactive serving bowl. Taste the hollandaise and adjust the seasoning, if necessary. If the hollandaise has gotten too thick, you can thin it by adding a teaspoon or two of lukewarm water. Serve the Hollandaise immediately, either poured over the broccoli or in a serving bowl for dipping.

SUPER-CHEESY RISOTTO

(rih-SAW-toh)

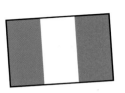

This is one of my all-time favorite Italian dishes ever! One taste, and it will change the way you think about rice—trust me. Now, risotto is made from a particular type of rice, so don't try this dish with regular long-grain rice, because it just won't work the same. The rice is also cooked in a unique way and results in a soft, creamy dish that is truly special. Just make sure to use the appropriate rice and follow the directions below. This dish goes well with just about anything I can think of! Feel free to kick yours up by stirring in your favorite sautéed veggies at the end, if the spirit moves you. Green peas and sautéed mushrooms are delicious additions.

INGREDIENTS

6 cups reduced-sodium chicken broth

2 tablespoons unsalted butter

2 tablespoons olive oil

1 medium yellow onion, finely chopped

1½ cups Italian risotto rice, such as arborio, carnaroli or vialone nano

1 teaspoon minced garlic

1 teaspoon white wine vinegar

½ teaspoon salt

¼ teaspoon ground white pepper

¼ cup heavy cream

1 cup finely grated Parmesan cheese, plus more for garnish (optional)

Freshly ground black pepper, for garnish (optional)

TOOLS

Measuring cups and spoons • cutting board • chef's knife • can opener (optional) • small saucepan • 4- to 5-quart heavy nonstick saucepan • wooden spoon • ladle • box grater • oven mitts or pot holders

DIRECTIONS

CAUTION

1. Add the chicken broth to a small saucepan and bring to a simmer.

2. In a 4- to 5-quart heavy nonstick saucepan over medium-high heat, melt the butter with the olive oil. Add the onion and cook, stirring occasionally, until the onion is soft and translucent, 3 to 4 minutes. Do not allow the onion to brown.

3. Add the rice and garlic and cook, stirring constantly, until the grains turn white and opaque and smell nutty and the garlic is fragrant, about 2 minutes. Add the vinegar, salt and pepper, and stir to combine.

4. Using a ladle, begin adding the hot broth mixture to the saucepan, one ladle at a time, stirring frequently and not adding more liquid until the prior addition is completely absorbed by the rice. The rice should take about 18 to 20 minutes to cook, and you might not need quite all of the liquid. (Or, if you have used all of the broth and the rice is still not cooked through, add a bit of hot water.) The rice should be very smooth and creamy, and the grains should be separate and tender without being mushy.

STEP 4

5. When the rice has reached the proper consistency, remove the saucepan from the heat and add the heavy cream and the Parmesan cheese. Stir to combine well and serve immediately, garnished with additional Parmesan cheese and a pinch of freshly grated black pepper, if desired.

AFRICAN-INSPIRED SWEET POTATO PUREE

This sweet potato puree is flavored with cane syrup, lemon, and ginger—three flavors that are used often in West African cooking. This dish makes a wonderful accompaniment to the BBQ Ribs (page 126), the Puerto Rican Roast Pork (page 122), or even a simple roast chicken or turkey.

DID YOU KNOW . . .

Though we use sweet potatoes for this dish, in Africa they would use native yams, which are a different plant species and harder to find in the U.S.

INGREDIENTS

3 pounds sweet potatoes, peeled and cut into 1-inch cubes

$\frac{1}{2}$ cup dark cane syrup or molasses

4 tablespoons unsalted butter, softened

$\frac{1}{4}$ cup heavy cream

1 tablespoon fresh lemon juice

$1\frac{1}{4}$ teaspoons ground ginger

$\frac{3}{4}$ teaspoon lemon zest

$\frac{1}{8}$ teaspoon salt

Pinch of ground black pepper

TOOLS

Measuring cups and spoons • cutting board • chef's knife • vegetable peeler • zester or box grater • medium saucepan • fork • colander • food processor • wooden spoon • oven mitts or pot holders

DIRECTIONS   CAUTION

1. Place the peeled, cut sweet potatoes in a medium saucepan and add enough cold water to cover by 2 inches. Bring to a boil over high heat. Reduce the heat so that the potatoes remain at a low boil, and cook until fork-tender, about 10 minutes. Drain in a colander placed in the sink.

2. Transfer the potatoes to the bowl of a food processor along with all of the remaining ingredients, and process until fairly smooth, 1 to 2 minutes. Return the potato puree to the saucepan and warm gently over low heat, stirring frequently, before serving.

Note: If you like a chunkier consistency or if you do not have a food processor, the potatoes may be mashed with a potato masher instead.

PORTUGUESE RICE

 This is a popular way to prepare rice in Portugal—but it also has similarities to Spanish and Mexican rice. This dish makes a wonderful side to any meal—poultry, meat, or seafood. If you're not a fan of cilantro, simply substitute an equal amount of parsley. Serve it any time you would normally serve plain white rice for something to tantalize your taste buds!

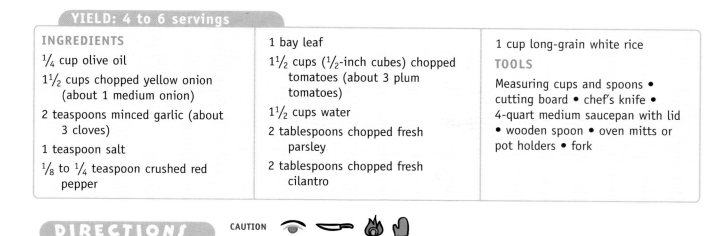

INGREDIENTS

¼ cup olive oil

1½ cups chopped yellow onion (about 1 medium onion)

2 teaspoons minced garlic (about 3 cloves)

1 teaspoon salt

⅛ to ¼ teaspoon crushed red pepper

1 bay leaf

1½ cups (½-inch cubes) chopped tomatoes (about 3 plum tomatoes)

1½ cups water

2 tablespoons chopped fresh parsley

2 tablespoons chopped fresh cilantro

1 cup long-grain white rice

TOOLS

Measuring cups and spoons • cutting board • chef's knife • 4-quart medium saucepan with lid • wooden spoon • oven mitts or pot holders • fork

DIRECTIONS   CAUTION

1. In a 4-quart medium saucepan, heat the olive oil over high heat until hot.

2. Add the onion and cook, stirring, until softened, 4 minutes.

3. Add the garlic, salt, crushed red pepper, and bay leaf and cook, stirring, for 1 minute.

4. Add the tomatoes and cook, stirring occasionally, until they begin to soften, about 2 minutes.

5. Add the water, parsley, and cilantro and bring to a boil.

6. Add the rice and stir well. When the liquid returns to a boil, stir once again, cover the pot, and reduce the heat to low. Cook the rice, undisturbed, for 20 minutes, until the liquid is dissolved and the rice is tender.

7. Let the rice stand for 5 minutes before fluffing with a fork. Remove the bay leaf and serve immediately.

REFRIED BEANS

This popular Mexican dish turns simple cooked beans into an awesome side dish. It makes a wonderful addition to a plate of enchiladas, especially when paired with the Portuguese Rice on page 144. Or, whip up a batch to serve as the filling for tacos, tostadas, or burritos. Olé!

INGREDIENTS

½ pound (1¼ cups) dried pinto beans, rinsed and picked over (page 14)

1 bay leaf

1 yellow onion, halved, one half cut in 2 pieces and the other half chopped

2 garlic cloves, peeled and smashed, plus 1 teaspoon minced garlic

2 teaspoons salt

3 tablespoons vegetable oil or bacon drippings

¼ teaspoon ground cumin

¼ teaspoon dried oregano

1 tablespoon extra-virgin olive oil

Grated Cheddar or Monterey Jack cheese, for serving (optional)

Chopped tomatoes, for serving (optional)

Sour cream, for serving (optional)

Chopped chives, for serving (optional)

TOOLS

Measuring cups and spoons • cutting board • chef's knife • box grater (optional) • medium saucepan with lid • wooden spoon • colander • medium bowl • medium 10-inch skillet • oven mitts or pot holders • potato masher

DIRECTIONS

CAUTION

1. In a medium saucepan, combine the beans, bay leaf, two onion quarters, smashed garlic, and enough water to cover by 2 inches, and bring to a boil. Reduce the heat so that the water boils gently and cook for 10 minutes. Cover, remove from the heat, and allow the beans to sit for 1 hour.

2. After 1 hour, return the beans to a low boil and cook, stirring occasionally, until they begin to soften, about 45 minutes. Add the salt and continue to cook until the beans are very tender, about 15 to 30 minutes longer. Drain the beans in a colander set over a bowl in the sink and reserve the cooking liquid. Discard the bay leaf, onion half, and garlic.

3. In a medium 10-inch skillet, heat the vegetable oil over medium-high heat. Add the chopped onion and cook until soft, stirring occasionally, about 4 minutes.

4. Add the minced garlic, cumin, and oregano, and cook for 1 minute.

5. Add the beans and 1 cup of the reserved cooking liquid and, using a potato masher, mash the beans until chunky-smooth. Add ¾ cup more of the reserved cooking liquid and cook, stirring, until the beans are very thick and flavorful, about 10 minutes. Be careful of splatters! If the beans become too thick, simply add a little more of the reserved cooking liquid. When the beans have reached the desired consistency, stir in the olive oil and serve immediately. The beans are delicious on their own, or kick yours up by topping with any or all of the following optional items: grated cheese, chopped tomatoes, sour cream, and/or chopped chives.

STEP 5

Note: These beans can be made several days in advance and reheated before serving—just keep in mind that you may need to add a bit more liquid when reheating, as they tend to thicken as they sit and cool.

6

CHAPTER

CHALLAH

(HAH-lah)

This deliciously soft, moist bread is eaten all over Eastern Europe, particularly as part of traditional Jewish meals. Try some toasted with butter and jam for breakfast, or make a grilled cheese on thin slices for a yummy lunch treat. And hey, this bread also makes killer French toast!

DIRECTIONS

CAUTION

1. Combine the yeast, sugar, and warm milk in the bowl of a standing electric mixer. Stir with a wooden spoon and let stand for 10 to 15 minutes, until the surface appears foamy.

2. Stir in the melted butter and 3 of the eggs and stir until thoroughly combined. Fit the mixer with the paddle attachment and place the mixing bowl on the mixer.

3. Sift the flour and salt into a medium mixing bowl.

4. With the mixer running on low speed, carefully add 3½ cups of the flour, one cup at a time, until a soft, sticky dough is formed.

CAUTION

Be careful to keep utensils and fingers away from the rotating beaters of the mixer when adding ingredients.

150

INGREDIENTS

2 (¼-ounce) packets active dry yeast

⅓ cup sugar

1 cup warm milk (100° to 110°F on an instant-read thermometer)

6 tablespoons unsalted butter, melted

4 large eggs

4¼ cups all-purpose flour

2 teaspoons salt

2 teaspoons vegetable oil

TOOLS

Measuring cups and spoons • small saucepan • instant-read thermometer • standing electric mixer with paddle attachment • wooden spoon • sifter • medium mixing bowl • large mixing bowl • plastic wrap or clean, damp kitchen towel • parchment paper • large baking sheet • small mixing bowl • fork • pastry brush • oven mitts or pot holders

Be careful to stay clear of the rotating paddle! Add the remaining flour in ¼-cup increments. You may not need all of the flour. To know whether you have added enough flour, test the dough by turning off the mixer and touching the dough with your finger. It should remain slightly sticky and not at all dry. If it's getting dry and very stiff, do not add any more flour.

STEP 4

5. Increase the mixer speed to medium-low and allow the paddle to knead the dough until the dough is very smooth and elastic, about 5 minutes.

6. Grease a large mixing bowl with the oil and add the dough to the bowl. Turn the dough so that it is coated with oil. Then cover the dough with plastic wrap or a clean, damp kitchen towel, and let it stand in a warm, draft-free place to rise until doubled in size, 1 to 1½ hours.

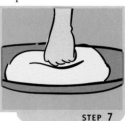

STEP 7

7. Punch the dough down with your fist before turning it out onto a clean work surface, and then divide it into 3 equal portions. Using your palms, start in the center and work outward, rolling each portion of dough gently against the work surface with even pressure to form a rope about 20 inches long. Repeat with the rest of the dough.

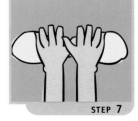

STEP 7

8. Press the 3 ropes together at one end to seal. Lay the 3 ropes next to one another, with the sealed end farthest away from you. Begin braiding the loaf by crossing one of the outer ropes over the center rope. Continue to braid by crossing alternating outer ropes, one at a time, over the center rope. When the ropes are completely braided, press the ends of the 3 ropes together and transfer the loaf to a parchment-lined baking sheet. Tuck the pinched portions of the ends under slightly so that they are not visible. Cover with plastic wrap or a clean, damp kitchen towel and set aside in a warm place until loaf has doubled in size, about 30 minutes.

STEP 8

9. Position rack in bottom third of oven and preheat the oven to 375°F.

10 Place the remaining egg in a small mixing bowl and beat lightly with a fork. Using a pastry brush, coat the entire top and sides of the loaf with the eggwash. Bake for 10 minutes, then reduce the heat to 350°F. Continue to bake for an additional 15 to 20 minutes, until the loaf is golden brown and the bread sounds hollow when tapped on the top. Using oven mitts or pot holders, remove the baking sheet from the oven. Let cool before slicing.

HOT CROSS BUNS

 These are favorites in the British Isles and are traditionally made around Easter. But they are tasty any time of the year. At my house we like to add raisins, but you can substitute other kinds of dried fruit, such as cherries or cranberries, if you prefer. Make sure you wait until the buns are cooled to drizzle the icing or it will not stick to the buns.

DiD YOU KNOW . . .

Some say these buns date back to the twelfth century, when an Anglican monk was said to have put the sign of the cross on the buns to honor Good Friday. Others say they have their roots in pagan spring festivals.

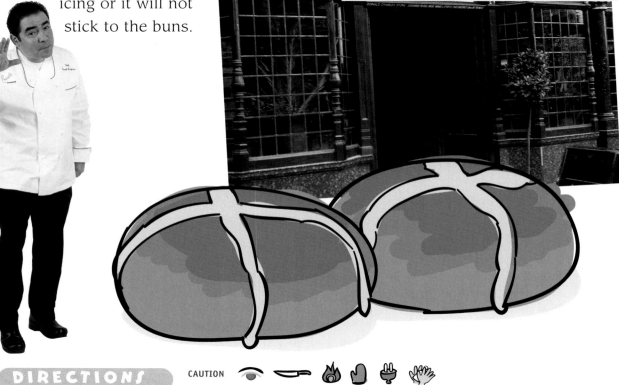

DIRECTIONS

CAUTION

1. Stir the yeast and granulated sugar into the warm milk. Allow the mixture to stand 10 minutes until it becomes foamy.

2. Combine the flour, brown sugar, cinnamon, cloves, allspice, nutmeg, salt, and orange zest in the bowl of a standing electric mixer fitted with the paddle attachment. Mix on low to combine.

3. Pour the milk and yeast mixture into the flour mixture and beat on low to combine.

4. With the mixer running, carefully add 2 of the eggs, one at a time, mixing just until the yolks disappear, keeping your fingers away from the rotating paddle.

CAUTION Be careful to keep utensils and fingers away from the rotating beaters of the mixer when adding ingredients.

152

INGREDIENTS

1 (1/4-ounce) packet active dry yeast

1/2 teaspoon granulated sugar

3/4 cup warm milk (100° to 110°F on an instant-read thermometer)

3 3/4 cups all-purpose flour

1/4 cup light brown sugar

1 teaspoon ground cinnamon

1/4 teaspoon ground cloves

1/4 teaspoon ground allspice

1/4 teaspoon ground nutmeg

1/2 teaspoon salt

1 1/2 teaspoons freshly grated orange zest

3 large eggs

1/4 cup unsalted butter, softened

1/2 cup raisins

2 teaspoons vegetable oil, for greasing a large mixing bowl

2 tablespoons milk

1/2 cup confectioners' sugar

TOOLS

Measuring cups and spoons • citrus zester, microplane, or grater • small saucepan • instant-read thermometer • standing electric mixer with paddle attachment • small mixing bowl • large mixing bowl • plastic wrap or clean, damp kitchen towel • baking sheet • parchment paper • whisk • 2 small mixing bowls • pastry brush • oven mitts or pot holders • spatula • wire rack • squeeze bottle with small tip or plastic bag

5. Add the softened butter and the raisins and mix until the dough is smooth and elastic, about 4 minutes.

6. Grease a large mixing bowl with the oil. Place the dough in the lightly greased bowl and turn the dough once to coat it with the oil. Cover with plastic wrap or a clean, damp kitchen towel and set in a warm, draft-free place to rise until doubled in size, about 1 1/2 hours.

7. Position rack in center of oven and preheat the oven to 400°F. Line a baking sheet with parchment paper.

8. When the dough has risen, punch it down once with your fist and turn the dough out onto a lightly floured surface. Divide the dough into 12 equal pieces and form each piece into a round ball.

STEP 8

9. Evenly space each dough ball on the prepared baking sheet.

10. Whisk together the remaining egg and 1 tablespoon of the milk in a small mixing bowl. Using a pastry brush, paint the top of each roll with the egg mixture, reserving the remaining eggwash. Place a clean, damp kitchen towel or lightly greased piece of plastic wrap over the tops of the rolls. Set in a warm place to rise, about 30 minutes.

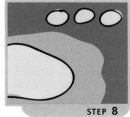

STEP 8

11. Remove the kitchen towel and brush the tops of the rolls again with the reserved eggwash.

12. Bake for 10 to 15 minutes until golden brown.

13. Using oven mitts or pot holders, remove the baking sheet from the oven. Use a spatula to remove the rolls from the baking sheet and place them on a wire rack to cool.

14. In a clean small mixing bowl, combine the confectioners' sugar and remaining tablespoon of milk, mixing well. Pour the sugar glaze into a squeeze bottle with a small tip or into a plastic bag with a small hole cut in one of the corners.

STEP 15

15. When the rolls have cooled completely, pipe the sugar glaze over the top of each roll in the shape of a cross.

MEXICAN CORNBREAD

 I've added the flavors of Mexico to this quick bread. If you like a little more spice, try adding Pepper Jack cheese in place of the Monterey Jack. Cornbread is best eaten hot, but I have to say that I enjoy eating it cool as an afternoon snack as well.

DID YOU KNOW . . .

Native Americans were making cornbread long before the first European settlers arrived in the Americas. The earliest cornbread was called "pone" from the Algonquian word "apan."

INGREDIENTS

2 tablespoons unsalted butter

1½ cups chopped yellow onion (about 1 medium onion)

1 teaspoon minced garlic (about 2 cloves)

1 small red bell pepper, seeded and chopped (about ¾ cup)

1 jalapeño, seeded and finely chopped

1 cup fresh or frozen corn kernels (see page 17)

1¼ teaspoons salt

¼ cup vegetable oil or bacon grease

1 cup all-purpose flour

1 cup yellow cornmeal

2 teaspoons baking powder

½ teaspoon sugar

¾ cup grated Monterey Jack cheese

2 large eggs

1 cup buttermilk

TOOLS

Measuring cups and spoons • cutting board • chef's knife • rubber gloves • box grater • large nonstick skillet • wooden spoon • 9-inch cast-iron skillet or other heavy ovenproof skillet • medium mixing bowl • whisk • oven mitts or pot holders

DIRECTIONS   CAUTION

1. Position rack in center of oven and preheat the oven to 400°F.

2. Melt the butter in a large nonstick skillet over medium heat. Add onion, garlic, red bell pepper, jalapeño, and corn. Cook, stirring occasionally, for 10 minutes, until the vegetables are softened. Add ¼ teaspoon of the salt to the vegetables. Remove from the heat and cool.

   > **CAUTION** Always handle jalapeño peppers with rubber gloves and be careful not to touch your eyes or skin.

3. Pour 2 tablespoons of the oil or bacon grease into a 9-inch cast-iron skillet. Place the skillet in the preheated oven for 10 minutes.

4. In a medium mixing bowl, stir together the flour, cornmeal, baking powder, sugar, and the remaining 1 teaspoon of salt.

5. Add the cheese, cooled vegetables, eggs, buttermilk, and remaining 2 tablespoons of oil or bacon grease to the flour mixture. Whisk until just combined—do not overmix.

6. Using oven mitts or pot holders, carefully remove the hot skillet from the oven. Carefully pour the cornmeal batter into the hot skillet, making sure that the hot grease does not splash out.

7. Using oven mitts or pot holders, return the skillet to the oven. Bake for 25 to 30 minutes, until golden brown and cooked through.

8. Using oven mitts or pot holders, remove the cornbread from the oven and allow to sit for a few minutes before cutting into wedges and serving.

INDIAN NAAN BREAD

(NAHN)

This bread from India is similar to pita bread. If you haven't tried it before, I bet you'll like it! It's super easy to make, too, so whip up a batch next time you're having friends over for a party. Cut it into strips or wedges and serve it with your favorite dip or spread. It's great with the Herbed Mediterranean Yogurt Cheese Spread on page 58 or served alongside the Vegetable Curry on page 108.

INGREDIENTS

1 teaspoon active dry yeast

$1/2$ teaspoon sugar

$1/2$ cup warm water (100° to 110°F on an instant-read thermometer)

$1^1/4$ cups all-purpose flour, plus more for kneading dough

$1/2$ teaspoon salt

$1/4$ cup plus 1 teaspoon clarified butter (still warm) (page 21)

TOOLS

Measuring cups and spoons • glass measuring cup • instant-read thermometer • spoon • sifter • large mixing bowl • small mixing bowl • plastic wrap or clean, damp kitchen towel • large baking sheet • rolling pin • oven mitts or pot holders

DIRECTIONS   CAUTION 👁 🔥 🧤

1. In a glass measuring cup, combine the yeast and sugar. Add the warm water and stir well. Let the mixture rest until foamy, 5 to 10 minutes.

2. Sift together the flour and salt into a large mixing bowl. Make a well in the center of the flour with clean hands and pour the yeast mixture and $1/4$ cup of the clarified butter into the center. Mix together with your fingers until a smooth dough forms. The dough should be slightly sticky. You can add a small amount of extra flour if needed.

STEP 2

3. Transfer the dough to a lightly floured surface and knead for 3 minutes.

4. Oil a small mixing bowl with the remaining teaspoon of butter and place the dough in the bowl, turning to coat. Cover the bowl with plastic wrap or a clean, damp kitchen towel and let rest in a warm, draft-free place to rise until doubled in size, about 1 hour.

5. Position rack in center of oven and preheat the oven to 400°F. Lightly grease a large baking sheet.

6. Divide the dough into 6 equal pieces and transfer to a lightly floured work surface. Using a lightly floured rolling pin, gently roll each portion of dough into a circle about 5 or 6 inches in diameter.

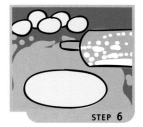
STEP 6

7. Transfer the dough circles to the prepared baking sheet and bake until just golden brown and puffed, 12 to 15 minutes.

8. Using oven mitts or pot holders, remove the baking sheet from the oven. Serve immediately.

STEP 7

HOT DOG BUNS

 It's estimated that during the Fourth of July celebrations, Americans eat about 150 million hot dogs! To make a good thing great, try these homemade buns and your family picnics will never be the same. Not only does this recipe make great hot dog buns, but you can use the dough to make hamburger buns as well. Just shape the dough into small round loaves instead of log shapes.

DID YOU KNOW . . .

Some say a German butcher named Charles Feltman opened the first Coney Island hot dog stand in 1871, selling "dachshund" sausages.

 **DIRECTIONS**   CAUTION

1. In a small mixing bowl, add the yeast to the warm water and sprinkle with 1 pinch of sugar. Let the mixture stand for 10 minutes, until foamy.

2. In a large mixing bowl, combine the remaining sugar, flour, and salt. Using a wooden spoon, stir to combine.

3. Using your fingers, a fork, or a pastry cutter, mix the butter pieces into the flour mixture until it resembles coarse crumbs.

4. Add the yeast mixture, the warm milk, and ½ cup of the olive oil to the flour mixture. Continue mixing until all the ingredients come together to form a soft dough. If the mixture is too wet, add ¼ cup more flour until the dough comes together.

STEP **3**

158

INGREDIENTS

1 (1¼ ounce) packet active dry yeast

½ cup warm water (100° to 110°F on an instant-read thermometer)

1 pinch plus 1 tablespoon sugar

3¼ cups all-purpose flour

1 teaspoon kosher salt

2 tablespoons unsalted butter, cut into pieces

½ cup warm milk (100° to 110°F on an instant-read thermometer)

½ cup plus 2 teaspoons olive oil

1 large egg, lightly beaten

2 tablespoons heavy cream

TOOLS

Measuring cups and spoons • small mixing bowl • instant-read thermometer • 2 large mixing bowls • wooden spoon • fork or pastry cutter • plastic wrap or clean, damp kitchen towel • knife • baking sheet • parchment paper • 2 small mixing bowls • whisk • pastry brush • oven mitts or pot holders • spatula • wire rack • toothpick • serrated knife

5. Turn the dough out onto a lightly floured surface and knead for 3 to 5 minutes, until the dough is smooth and elastic. You may need to continue adding a light dusting of flour to your work surface to keep the dough from sticking. (This dough is very soft.)

6. Grease a second large mixing bowl with the remaining 2 teaspoons of olive oil and place the dough in the bowl, turning to coat with the oil.

7. Cover the bowl with a clean, damp kitchen towel or plastic wrap and set in a warm, draft-free place to rise until the dough has doubled in size, about 1 hour.

8. Punch the dough down in the center with your fist and turn it out onto a lightly floured surface.

STEP 8

9. Divide the dough into 8 equal portions, about 3½ ounces each.

10. Using your clean hands, press each portion of dough to flatten, then gently roll into a log shape, about 5 inches long.

STEP 10

11. Place each log on a baking sheet lined with parchment paper that has been lightly sprinkled with flour.

12. In a small mixing bowl, whisk together the egg and cream. Using a pastry brush, gently paint the eggwash onto the top of each bun.

13. Cover the baking sheet with a clean, damp kitchen towel or lightly greased plastic wrap and set in a warm, draft-free place to rise until the rolls double in size, about 1 hour.

14. Position rack in lower third of oven and preheat the oven to 375°F.

15. Remove the kitchen towel or plastic wrap and bake for 20 to 30 minutes, until the tops are golden brown and a toothpick inserted into the dough comes out clean. Use oven mitts or pot holders to remove the baking sheet from the oven.

16. Using a spatula, move the rolls to a wire rack to cool completely.

17. To serve, slice the buns horizontally with a serrated knife about three-fourths of the way through.

COCONUT BREAD

 This Cuban quick bread is so good, you might want to eat it for dessert! Because coconuts are so widely available in Cuba and other Caribbean, Central, and South American countries, they're used in many of the Cuban native dishes. This is one of my very favorites!

INGREDIENTS

1 tablespoon plus ½ cup unsalted butter

2½ cups all-purpose flour

¾ cup sugar

1 tablespoon baking powder

¼ teaspoon salt

1 (6-ounce) package frozen fresh coconut flakes, thawed, or sweetened flaked coconut (about 1⅓ cups, packed)

1¼ cups coconut milk

2 large eggs

½ teaspoon vanilla extract

TOOLS

Measuring cups and spoons • 9 x 5-inch loaf pan • 2 large mixing bowls • spoon • knife • pastry cutter (optional) • whisk • toothpick • oven mitts or pot holders • wire rack

DIRECTIONS

CAUTION

1. Position rack in bottom third of oven and preheat the oven to 350°F.

2. Grease a 9 by 5-inch loaf pan with 1 tablespoon of the butter. Set aside.

3. In a large mixing bowl, combine the flour, sugar, baking powder, and salt. Stir to combine.

4. Using a knife, cut the remaining butter into small cubes. Using a pastry cutter or your fingers, blend the butter into the flour mixture until it resembles coarse meal.

STEP 4

5. Add the coconut, stirring to combine.

6. In a second large mixing bowl, whisk together the coconut milk, eggs, and vanilla.

7. Using your clean hands, make a well in the flour mixture and pour the milk mixture into it, stirring just until moistened. The batter will be lumpy.

STEP 7

8. Pour the batter into the prepared baking pan and bake for 1 hour and 5 minutes to 1 hour and 10 minutes, until a toothpick inserted into the center comes out clean.

9. Using oven mitts or pot holders, remove the pan from the oven. Allow the bread to cool in the pan for 10 minutes. Invert the bread onto a wire rack to cool. Serve warm or at room temperature.

CHAPTER 7

LEMONY PANNA COTTA (PAHN-nah KOH-tah) WITH BLUEBERRY SAUCE

Our version of this Italian dessert, whose name translates as "cooked cream," is made from milk and heavy cream that has been flavored with a light lemony tang. This dessert is quick and easy, and is great to make ahead of time because it will keep for up to 1 week in the refrigerator. The Blueberry Sauce really adds the perfect touch—so don't even think of skipping it!

DIRECTIONS

CAUTION 👁 🔪 🔥 🧤

1. Lightly spray six ¾-cup ramekins or custard cups with nonstick cooking spray and set aside.

2. In a heavy medium saucepan, combine the cream and milk. Using the tip of a small, sharp paring knife, scrape the seeds from the vanilla bean into the saucepan and add the scraped pod. Bring to a simmer over medium heat. Remove the saucepan from the heat and add the lemon zest. Cover and let the milk mixture steep for 30 minutes. Strain the mixture through a fine-mesh sieve into a small mixing bowl and discard the solids. Return the mixture to the saucepan.

STEP 2

3. Combine the lemon juice and gelatin in a small mixing bowl and let stand until the gelatin softens, about 10 minutes.

4. Add the gelatin mixture and the sugar to the cream mixture in the saucepan. Heat over low heat, stirring with a wooden spoon, until the gelatin and sugar are dissolved, about 2 minutes. Remove from the heat and whisk in the crème fraiche.

5. Carefully divide the mixture evenly among the prepared ramekins or custard cups. Allow to cool to room temperature, then cover with plastic wrap and refrigerate until thoroughly set, at least 6 hours or overnight.

6. When you are ready to serve, run the paring knife around the edge of each custard. Carefully dip the bottom of each ramekin into a medium bowl filled with hot water for 15 to 20 seconds to loosen the custard, but keep your fingers out of the hot water! Place a small dessert plate onto the top of the ramekin. While holding the plate and ramekin together, invert both, shaking gently to help release the custard from the ramekin onto the plate.

STEP 6

7. Serve with the Blueberry Sauce spooned over the top.

INGREDIENTS

Nonstick cooking spray

1¼ cups heavy cream

¾ cup whole milk

½ vanilla bean, split lengthwise

½ teaspoon lemon zest

5 tablespoons fresh lemon juice

2 teaspoons unflavored gelatin

½ cup sugar

½ cup crème fraiche

Blueberry Sauce (recipe follows)

TOOLS

Measuring cups and spoons • six ¾-cup ramekins or custard cups •

heavy medium saucepan with lid • paring knife • zester (optional) • fine-mesh sieve • 2 small mixing bowls • juicer (optional) • wooden spoon • whisk • plastic wrap • oven mitts or pot holders • medium bowl • 6 small dessert plates

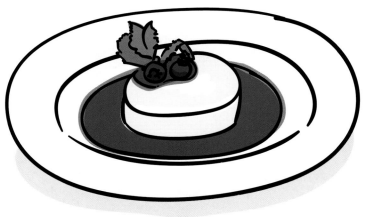

BLUEBERRY SAUCE

This sauce can be made ahead of time and kept in the refrigerator for up to 1 week and then allowed to come to room temperature just before serving. Fresh blueberries can be substituted for frozen.

INGREDIENTS

1 (16-ounce) package frozen blueberries, thawed

4 (½-inch-wide) lemon zest strips

⅓ cup sugar

½ cup plus 1 tablespoon water

1 tablespoon cornstarch

TOOLS

Measuring cups and spoons • vegetable peeler • medium

saucepan • wire-mesh strainer • medium mixing bowl • wooden spoon • small mixing bowl • whisk • oven mitts or pot holders

DIRECTIONS   CAUTION

1. Combine blueberries, strips of lemon zest, sugar, and ½ cup of water in a medium saucepan. Bring the berry mixture to a boil over medium-high heat. Reduce the heat to medium-low and simmer for 5 minutes. Remove from heat.

2. Place a wire-mesh strainer over a medium mixing bowl and pour the blueberry mixture into the strainer. Using a wooden spoon, gently mash the blueberries to release all of the liquid, discarding the skins when done. Pour the sauce back into the saucepan.

STEP 2

3. In a small mixing bowl, combine the cornstarch and 1 tablespoon of water, whisking until smooth.

4. Pour the cornstarch mixture into the blueberry sauce, whisking or stirring to combine. Bring the sauce to a boil over medium-high heat, stirring constantly, and allow to boil for 1 minute.

5. Remove the sauce from the heat and cool to room temperature.

6. Serve with the Lemony Panna Cotta.

AUSTRALIAN PAVLOVAS WITH FRESH BERRIES AND STRAWBERRY PUREE

(pav-LOH-vuhs)

Australians were so impressed with Russian ballerina Anna Pavlova's dancing that they named these lighter-than-air treats after her. Meringue cakes existed in Australia and New Zealand before Pavlova's tour in 1929, but the name for this dessert seems just perfect. These individual pavlovas are inspired by the larger version served in Australia.

CAUTION Be careful to keep utensils and fingers away from the rotating beaters of the mixer when adding ingredients.

DIRECTIONS   CAUTION   👁 🔪 🔥 🧤 🔌 ✋

1. Position rack in bottom third of oven and preheat the oven to 200°F. Line 2 large baking sheets with aluminum foil.

2. Using a small saucer or the rim of a large glass, trace three 4-inch diameter circles onto the foil on each baking sheet using a food-safe, waterproof marker or pencil. Lightly butter the foil. Set the baking sheets aside.

STEP 2

3. In the bowl of a standing electric mixer, beat the egg whites and cream of tartar on medium speed until foamy. Carefully begin adding the superfine sugar, one tablespoon at a time, and increase the speed to medium-high. Continue to beat until the egg whites are stiff and glossy, about 7 minutes. Turn the mixer off and, using a spatula, transfer the meringue to a pastry bag fitted with a ½-inch plain tip. See page 23 for an alternative piping method.

STEP 3

INGREDIENTS

Butter, for greasing the foil

4 large egg whites, at room temperature

$1/4$ teaspoon cream of tartar

1 cup superfine sugar

3 tablespoons confectioners' sugar

4 cups strawberries, hulled and halved or quartered if large

3 tablespoons granulated sugar

1 tablespoon lemon juice

1 cup heavy cream

$1/2$ teaspoon vanilla extract

1 cup fresh raspberries, washed, picked over, and patted dry

1 cup fresh blueberries, washed, picked over, and patted dry

TOOLS

2 large baking sheets • aluminum foil • small saucer or large glass with a 4-inch diameter • food-safe waterproof marker or pencil • standing electric mixer • spatula • pastry bag fitted with a $1/2$-inch plain tip, or a plastic food storage bag • blender or food processor • 2 large spoons • fine-mesh sieve • medium mixing bowl • nonreactive measuring cup or small glass bowl • oven mitts or pot holders • small knife • airtight container (optional)

4. Using the traced circles on the foil as guides, carefully pipe concentric circles of the meringue onto the buttered foil so that the circles are completely filled with the meringue. Pipe a second and then a third ring of meringue around the top, outermost ring of each circle to form a shallow cup shape. Place 1 tablespoon of the confectioners' sugar in a fine-mesh sieve and shake the sugar evenly over the tops of the meringues.

STEP 4

5. Bake the meringues $1 1/2$ to 2 hours, until crisp. They will not color. Turn the oven off and leave the meringues in the oven to cool and continue crisping for at least 4 hours and up to overnight. They should feel very light. Remove the cool baking sheets from the oven and remove the meringue cups from the baking sheets by carefully peeling them off of the foil. Transfer to an airtight container, if storing. Meringues may be made up to several days in advance and kept in an airtight container until ready to serve.

6. Make the strawberry puree by combining 2 cups of the strawberries with the 3 tablespoons of granulated sugar and the lemon juice in a blender or food processor and blend until very smooth, about 2 minutes. Strain the mixture through a fine-mesh sieve into a medium mixing bowl and discard the solids. Transfer the sauce to a nonreactive measuring cup or small glass bowl and chill until ready to serve.

STEP 6

7. Place the cream in the bowl of an electric mixer and beat on medium-low until slightly thickened. Turn the mixer off and add the remaining 2 tablespoons confectioners' sugar. Beat on low speed until the sugar is incorporated and then increase the speed to medium-high. Continue to beat until stiff peaks form. Chill the whipped cream until ready to assemble the desserts.

8. When you are ready to serve, place each of the meringue cups on individual dessert plates and fill each cup with $2/3$ cup of the remaining assorted berries. Top each with $1/3$ cup of whipped cream and then spoon some of the strawberry sauce over the top of each dessert. Serve immediately.

STEP 8

TRES LECHES CAKE

(trays LEH-cheh)

 While this dessert is made in many South American countries, a Nicaraguan friend shared the recipe for this one with me. Tres leches means "three milks" in Spanish, so what makes this spongy cake unique is that it is soaked with three different kinds of milk. Best made a day ahead, with a little planning, it's perfect for your next party. A small portion of this rich concoction goes a long way!

DIRECTIONS   CAUTION

1. Position rack in bottom third of oven and preheat the oven to 350°F.

2. Lightly grease a 13 by 9-inch baking pan with 1 tablespoon of the shortening. Add 1 tablespoon of the flour to the greased pan and shake it around to coat the entire pan with the flour. Shake out excess flour. Set aside.

3. In the bowl of an electric mixer fitted with a whisk attachment, beat the egg whites on medium speed until soft peaks form. Reduce the speed to low and gradually add the sugar with the mixer running, beating until stiff peaks form.

INGREDIENTS

1 tablespoon vegetable shortening

1 tablespoon all-purpose flour

6 large eggs, separated

2 cups granulated sugar

2 cups all-purpose flour

2 teaspoons baking powder

$^1/_2$ cup whole milk

$1^1/_4$ teaspoons vanilla extract

1 (12-ounce) can evaporated milk

2 (14-ounce) cans sweetened condensed milk

3 cups heavy cream

1 tablespoon confectioners' sugar

TOOLS

Measuring cups and spoons • 13 x 9-inch baking pan • electric mixer fitted with whisk attachment • sifter • small mixing bowl • can opener • toothpick • oven mitts or pot holders • wire rack • blender

4. Add the egg yolks one at a time, beating well after each egg is added.

CAUTION Be careful to keep utensils and fingers away from the rotating beaters of the mixer when adding ingredients.

5. In a small mixing bowl, sift together the flour and baking powder.

6. Add the flour mixture to the batter in stages, alternating with the whole milk, beginning and ending with the flour. (Do this quickly so that the batter does not lose its volume.) Add 1 teaspoon of the vanilla extract. Pour the batter into the prepared pan and place in the oven.

7. Bake for 25 to 30 minutes, until a toothpick inserted into the center comes out clean.

8. Using oven mitts or pot holders, remove the cake from the oven and place on a wire rack to cool for 10 minutes.

9. In a blender, combine the evaporated milk, sweetened condensed milk, and 2 cups of the heavy cream. Replace the cover and blend on high for 45 seconds.

10. Remove $1^1/_2$ cups of the milk mixture, cover, and refrigerate until ready to serve the cake.

11. Pour half of the remaining milk mixture over the warm cake.

12. When the cake has soaked up most of the liquid, pour the remaining half of the milk mixture over the cake, and cool to room temperature. Cover and refrigerate until well chilled, at least 4 hours or overnight.

STEP 11

13. When ready to serve, beat the remaining cup of heavy cream in the electric mixer until soft peaks form. Add the confectioners' sugar and remaining $^1/_4$ teaspoon of vanilla, and beat until stiff peaks form. Spread the whipped cream over the chilled cake.

14. Serve the cake with the reserved chilled milk sauce.

CINNAMON-WALNUT SCOTTISH SHORTBREAD

The British Isles have always been known for their rich, buttery pastries, and Scottish shortbread has to be one of the best-known treats to come from this part of the world. Traditionally enjoyed in Scotland on New Year's Eve, shortbread is now served anywhere, anytime. Though it keeps well, don't count on having leftovers for long!

INGREDIENTS		
1 cup (2 sticks) unsalted butter, softened, plus a small amount for buttering the pan $\frac{1}{2}$ cup sugar $1\frac{1}{2}$ cups all-purpose flour	$\frac{1}{2}$ teaspoon ground cinnamon $\frac{1}{8}$ teaspoon allspice $\frac{1}{8}$ teaspoon salt $\frac{1}{2}$ cup finely chopped walnuts **TOOLS** Measuring cups and spoons •	two 9-inch round cake pans • standing electric mixer • sifter • medium mixing bowl • rubber spatula • fork • paring knife • oven mitts or pot holders • wire rack • airtight container • wax paper

DIRECTIONS   CAUTION 👁 🔪 🔥 🧤 🔌

1. Lightly butter two 9-inch round cake pans. Set aside.

2. In the bowl of an electric mixer, cream the butter and sugar on high speed until light and fluffy, 3 to 4 minutes.

   > **CAUTION** Be careful to keep your fingers and utensils away from rotating beaters when adding ingredients to a mixer.

3. Sift the flour, cinnamon, allspice, and salt into a medium mixing bowl.

4. With the mixer on low speed, carefully add the flour mixture and walnuts to the creamed butter mixture in 3 batches, waiting for each addition to be incorporated before adding the next. Continue mixing only until the flour is just incorporated—if you overmix, the shortbread will be tough.

5. Divide the dough evenly between the two prepared cake pans and, using your fingers, press the dough so that it forms a smooth layer covering the entire bottom surface of the cake pan. Using the tines of a fork, prick the pastry all over at regular intervals, pressing all the way through to the bottom. Press the tines of the fork all around the outer edges of the pan. Using a sharp paring knife, score the pastry rounds, cutting them only part of the way through to form 8 even wedges in each. Transfer the pans to the refrigerator to chill for at least 30 minutes before baking.

STEP 5

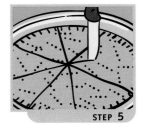

STEP 5

6. Position rack in center of oven and preheat the oven to 300°F.

7. Bake the shortbread until it is pale golden, 35 to 40 minutes.

8. Using oven mitts or pot holders, remove the pans from the oven. Cool the shortbread in the pans on a wire rack for 5 minutes. While the shortbread is still very warm, use a sharp knife to cut through the score marks all the way to the bottom of the pan.

9. Cool the shortbread completely, then carefully remove the wedges from the pans. Store the shortbread in an airtight container, layered with wax paper. Shortbread keeps very well but should be handled gently.

SUMMER PUDDING

This is a great summer dessert from England. For this version, we use strawberries, blueberries, blackberries and raspberries, but feel free to use your own favorite combination of berries. I have also found that if you need stale bread in a hurry, for this recipe it's best not to toast it in the oven. Just leave the bread slices out overnight on a baking sheet, uncovered, and your bread will be just right by the next day.

YIELD: 6 to 8 servings

INGREDIENTS

2 (8.8-ounce) containers fresh strawberries, washed, patted dry, hulled, and quartered (about 4 cups quartered berries)

2 (4.4-ounce) containers fresh blueberries, washed, picked over, and patted dry (about 2 cups)

½ pint fresh blackberries, washed, picked over, and patted dry (about 1 cup)

1 (6-ounce) container fresh raspberries, washed, picked over, and patted dry (about 1 cup)

¾ cup granulated sugar

2 tablespoons fresh lemon juice

10 to 12 slices stale white bread or challah bread, crusts removed

1 cup heavy cream

1 tablespoon confectioners' sugar

TOOLS

Measuring cups and spoons • juicer (optional) • large saucepan • oven mitts or pot holders • 9 x 5-inch loaf pan • plastic wrap • cutting board • bread knife • slotted spoon • spoon or ladle • small baking sheet or dish • 3 soup-size cans or other objects for weighting pudding • electric mixer fitted with whisk attachment • large serving platter

DIRECTIONS   CAUTION

1. Combine the strawberries, blueberries, blackberries, and raspberries in a large saucepan. Add the sugar and lemon juice and cook over medium heat until the fruit is tender and beginning to burst but still holds its shape, about 5 minutes. Using oven mitts or pot holders, remove the fruit from the heat and allow to cool to room temperature.

2. Meanwhile, line a 9 by 5-inch loaf pan with plastic wrap. Cut the bread slices (to fit in the bottom of the baking pan in the next step.) Repeat with the remaining bread slices as needed to fit into each layer. Set aside.

STEP 2

3. When the fruit has cooled, use a slotted spoon to place about 2 cups of the fruit in the bottom of the prepared baking pan, making sure the bottom is covered with fruit. Dip one side of the prepared bread slices in the juice from the cooked fruit, and place one layer of bread, soaked side down, on top of the fruit in the baking pan. Using a spoon or a ladle, spread enough juice on top of the bread layer so that none of the white is visible.

STEP 3

4. Repeat the fruit and bread layers two more times, ending with the bread layer. Pour any remaining juice on top of the last bread layer.

5. Cover tightly with plastic wrap and set the baking pan on a small baking sheet or dish. Place 3 soup-size cans on top of the wrapped pudding to weigh it down. Refrigerate the pudding with the can weights overnight.

6. In the bowl of an electric mixer fitted with a whisk attachment, add the heavy cream and confectioners' sugar and whisk until thick and frothy and stiff peaks have formed.

7. To serve, remove the can weights from the top of the pudding and carefully unwrap the plastic. Place a serving platter that is larger than the baking dish over the pudding and invert. Shake gently to release the pudding onto the serving platter and remove the plastic wrap.

8. Slice or spoon the summer pudding onto individual plates and serve chilled with the sweetened whipped cream.

BAKLAVA
(BAHK-lah-vah)

Hey, this delicious Greek dessert serves a crowd! I think you'll find that the little pieces of baklava, though rich, are intensely addictive. You'll be wanting more before you know it, which is okay because baklava will keep well, covered and at room temperature, for about 1 week!

DID YOU KNOW . . .

Some believe the Assyrians were the first to assemble layers of dough with fruit, nuts, and honey around the eighth century B.C. Then Greek seamen and merchants brought the recipe to Athens and perfected the phyllo technique for the dough. Phyllo means "leaf" in Greek.

DIRECTIONS   CAUTION 👁 ✎ 🔥 🧤

1. To make the syrup: Combine the sugar, honey, water, lemon juice, cinnamon sticks, lemon zest, cloves, and cardamom in a medium saucepan. Cook over medium heat, stirring occasionally with a wooden spoon, until the sugar has dissolved. Reduce the heat to medium-low and cook until the syrup is slightly thickened, about 10 minutes. Remove and discard the cinnamon sticks and lemon zest and set syrup aside to cool.

2. Using a chef's knife, finely chop the nuts. (Alternatively, if you have a food processor, pulse the nuts until finely chopped.) In a medium mixing bowl, combine the nuts, cinnamon, and salt and stir well to combine.

3. Melt the butter over low heat in a small saucepan.

4. Using a pastry brush, lightly coat a 13 by 9-inch or 15 by 10-inch baking dish with some of the melted butter.

INGREDIENTS	Filling and dough:	TOOLS
Syrup:	1 pound walnuts, or a combination of walnuts, pistachios, and almonds	Measuring cups and spoons • medium saucepan • wooden spoon • cutting board • chef's knife • food processor (optional) • medium mixing bowl • small saucepan • pastry brush • 13 x 9- or 15 x 10-inch baking dish • plastic wrap or damp kitchen towel • sharp knife • oven mitts or pot holders • wire rack • ladle or small measuring cup
1 cup sugar	1 teaspoon ground cinnamon	
1 cup honey	¼ teaspoon salt	
¾ cup water	2 sticks unsalted butter	
1 tablespoon fresh lemon juice	1 pound frozen phyllo, thawed according to package instructions	
2 cinnamon sticks		
1 (1-inch) strip of lemon zest		
Pinch of ground cloves		
Pinch of ground cardamom		

5. Open the package of thawed phyllo and lay the thin sheets on a clean work surface. Measure the phyllo sheets—if the type you have purchased measures approximately the same size as the baking dish you are using, then proceed from here. If they are larger than your baking dish, use a chef's knife to cut the phyllo sheets to approximately the same size as your baking dish. Discard any scraps. Cover the sheets with a piece of plastic wrap and a lightly damp kitchen towel, as the sheets of phyllo dry out very quickly if left uncovered. See page 23 for instructions on handling phyllo dough.

6. Position rack in center of oven and preheat the oven to 350°F.

7. Place one of the sheets of phyllo in the bottom of the buttered baking dish and lightly brush with some of the melted butter. Repeat this procedure with 6 more sheets of phyllo, for a total of 7 layers. Measure about ¾ cup of the nut mixture and spread the nut mixture evenly over the buttered phyllo sheets. Repeat with 7 more sheets of phyllo, buttering each layer as before, and top these sheets with another ¾ cup of the nut mixture. Continue this layering process until you have used all of the nut mixture. Layer any remaining sheets of phyllo on top, buttering between each layer, until all of the phyllo sheets have been used.

STEP 7

8. Use a sharp knife to make four cuts lengthwise through the layered phyllo at 1½-inch intervals. (You should end up with five lengthwise strips 1½ inches wide.) Now use your knife to cut diagonally across the strips at 1½-inch intervals to form diamond shapes. You should end up with approximately 36 diamond-shaped pieces of baklava in the baking dish.

9. Bake the baklava until golden brown, about 40 minutes.

STEP 8

10. Using oven mitts or pot holders, remove the baklava from the oven and set aside on a wire rack to cool for 5 minutes. Using a ladle or small measuring cup, slowly drizzle the cooled syrup over the warm baklava. Allow to stand several hours before serving.

STRAWBERRY-RHUBARB IRISH CRUMBLE

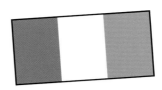

 Although fruit crisps and crumbles are made in several different countries, this one has a crunchy oatmeal topping and uses rhubarb, a vegetable often seen in Irish cooking. Fresh rhubarb peaks in late spring and early summer, which is perfect because it goes with the fresh strawberries that are harvested at the same time. If you're looking to make this dessert later in the year, try substituting frozen, sliced rhubarb.

INGREDIENTS

6 tablespoons cold unsalted butter, diced, plus 2 teaspoons for greasing the pan

5 cups strawberries, washed, hulled, and quartered

3 cups sliced rhubarb, about $\frac{1}{3}$ inch thick (fresh or frozen)

$\frac{1}{2}$ cup granulated sugar

$\frac{1}{4}$ cup cornstarch

1 teaspoon fresh lemon juice

$\frac{3}{4}$ cup all-purpose flour

$\frac{3}{4}$ cup old-fashioned rolled oats

$\frac{2}{3}$ cup packed light brown sugar

Pinch of salt

Vanilla ice cream (optional)

TOOLS

Measuring cups and spoons • cutting board • paring knife • juicer (optional) • 11 x 7-inch baking dish • 2 medium mixing bowls • wooden spoon • oven mitts or pot holders

DIRECTIONS

CAUTION

1. Position rack in center of oven and preheat the oven to 375°F. Lightly grease an 11 by 7-inch baking dish with 2 teaspoons of the butter and set aside.

2. In a medium mixing bowl, combine the strawberries, rhubarb, granulated sugar, cornstarch, and lemon juice. Toss to coat. Pour the strawberry-rhubarb mixture into the prepared baking dish.

3. In a second medium mixing bowl, add the flour, oats, light brown sugar, and salt, stirring to combine. Add the diced butter to the flour mixture and, using your fingers, work the mixture until it resembles coarse crumbs. Sprinkle the crumb mixture evenly on top of the strawberry mixture.

STEP 3

4. Place the baking dish in the oven and bake for 40 minutes, until the filling is bubbly and the topping is golden brown.

5. Using oven mitts or pot holders, remove the crumble from the oven and allow to cool for 10 minutes before serving.

6. Serve warm with vanilla ice cream, if desired.

ORANGE-SCENTED CHOCOLATE GELATO

(jeh-LAH-toh)

Gelato is the Italian word for ice cream. It is usually denser than the ice cream in America, and this chocolate gelato is super rich! Since making the gelato base is a little tricky for one person, you may need to grab a friend or family member so that one of you can ladle and pour and the other one can stir when tempering the egg mixture. If you're a fan of dark chocolate, try substituting bittersweet chocolate for the semisweet. This gelato is well worth the wait!

INGREDIENTS

1½ cups whole milk

1½ cups heavy cream

½ teaspoon grated orange zest

¾ cup superfine sugar

2 ounces good-quality semisweet chocolate, coarsely chopped

1 cup unsweetened cocoa powder

4 large egg yolks

TOOLS

Measuring cups and spoons • cutting board • chef's knife • citrus zester, microplane or grater • medium saucepan • 3 medium

mixing bowls • wire-mesh strainer • oven mitts or pot holders • whisk • large mixing bowl • ladle • instant-read thermometer • rubber spatula • wooden spoon • ice cream freezer • freezer-safe container

DIRECTIONS   CAUTION

1. Combine the milk, cream, orange zest, and ½ cup of the sugar in a medium saucepan over medium-low heat. Allow the mixture to come to a simmer, stirring to dissolve the sugar.

2. Place the chopped chocolate and the cocoa powder in a medium mixing bowl and set a wire-mesh strainer over the bowl.

3. Using oven mitts or pot holders, carefully pour the heated milk mixture through the strainer into the bowl. Whisk the milk and chocolate until the chocolate has completely melted and there are no lumps of chocolate or cocoa powder.

4. Fill a large mixing bowl about halfway with ice water and set aside.

5. In a second medium mixing bowl, combine the egg yolks and the remaining sugar. Whisk continuously until the mixture is pale yellow and slightly thickened, 3 to 4 minutes.

6. This is where you need two sets of hands. Using a ladle, slowly spoon the hot chocolate mixture into the egg mixture while another person is whisking the eggs continuously to keep them from cooking (curdling). Watch out here—it's hot! When all of the chocolate mixture has been whisked into the eggs, carefully return the mixture to the medium saucepan and set over medium-low heat. Stir the chocolate mixture constantly and cook until slightly thickened and an instant-read thermometer reaches 170°F.

> **CAUTION** When cooking and transferring the cream in steps 6 and 7, ask an adult for help because this mixture is really hot and sticky.

STEP 6

7. Using oven mitts or pot holders, remove the mixture from the heat and carefully pour immediately into a third medium mixing bowl. Carefully place the medium bowl in the large bowl of ice water to chill the mixture. Stir gently to cool with a wooden spoon, being careful not to let any of the ice water splash into the chocolate mixture. When the mixture has cooled, cover and refrigerate until thoroughly chilled, at least two hours and up to overnight.

8. Transfer the chocolate mixture to an ice cream freezer and freeze according to the manufacturer's directions.

STEP 8

9. Store the gelato in a freezer-safe container for at least 2 hours before serving.

NO-BAKE CARIBBEAN RICE PUDDING

Almost every country has its own version of this simple, comforting dish. Bring the flavors of the Caribbean islands to your kitchen by spicing this rice pudding with nutmeg, coconut, and cinnamon. This super-simple recipe can be prepared well in advance and served either warm or cold. My favorite way to enjoy it is warm, and sometimes I put a little whipped cream on top!

INGREDIENTS

2 cups water
2 pinches of salt
$\frac{1}{2}$ cup long-grain white rice
1 cup whole milk

$\frac{1}{2}$ cup coconut milk
$\frac{1}{4}$ cup golden raisins
$\frac{1}{4}$ cup sugar
2 tablespoons flaked coconut
$\frac{1}{8}$ teaspoon grated nutmeg

$\frac{1}{4}$ teaspoon ground cinnamon
$\frac{1}{2}$ teaspoon vanilla extract

TOOLS

Measuring cups and spoons • large heavy saucepan with lid • wooden spoon • oven mitts or pot holders

DIRECTIONS

CAUTION

1. Bring the water to a boil in a large heavy saucepan over high heat. Add the salt and the rice and stir to combine. Reduce the heat to low, cover, and simmer, stirring occasionally, until the rice is very tender, 25 to 30 minutes.

2. Add the milk, coconut milk, raisins, sugar, coconut, nutmeg, and cinnamon. Cook uncovered, stirring often, until most of the milk is absorbed, about 20 minutes.

3. Remove from the heat and add the vanilla. Stir to blend. Serve warm or chilled.

APRICOT-WALNUT RUGELACH

(RUHG-uh-luhkh)

These little cookies are great to eat any time of the day. They are made all over Eastern Europe and can be baked with many different fillings and flavorings. You're going to be surprised at how easy this dough is to work with.

DIRECTIONS CAUTION

1. Combine the softened butter and cream cheese in the bowl of a standing electric mixer fitted with a paddle attachment. Cream together on low speed for about 2 minutes, until smooth and creamy.

2. Continue mixing on low speed and gradually add the flour, sugar, and salt. Mix for 2 more minutes. Be careful here while the mixer is in motion!

CAUTION Be careful to keep utensils and fingers away from the rotating beaters of the mixer when adding ingredients.

182

INGREDIENTS

1 cup unsalted butter, softened

1 (8-ounce) package cream cheese, softened

2 cups all-purpose flour

1/3 cup confectioners' sugar

Pinch of salt

1½ cups apricot 100% fruit spread

2/3 cup chopped, toasted walnuts

3 tablespoons coarse or granulated sugar

TOOLS

Measuring cups and spoons • chef's knife • standing electric mixer with paddle attachment • plastic wrap • small mixing bowl • rolling pin • spatula or spoon • small paring knife or pizza wheel • parchment paper • baking sheet • oven mitts or pot holders

3. Turn the mixer off and remove the dough mixture from the bowl, wrap with plastic wrap and refrigerate for 2 to 3 hours. (This dough can be made a day ahead.)

4. In a small mixing bowl, combine the apricot fruit spread and the walnuts. Set aside.

5. When the dough has chilled, divide into 4 equal portions. You will only work with one portion at a time, so keep the rest in the refrigerator until ready to use.

6. Position rack in bottom third of oven and preheat the oven to 350°F.

7. On a lightly floured surface, use a rolling pin to roll one part of the dough into a circle, about 1/8 inch thick.

8. Using a spatula or the back of a spoon, spread one-fourth of the apricot filling onto the circle all the way to the edges. (You should have just enough for a thin layer of filling; it shouldn't be a thick coating.)

STEP 8

9. Using a small paring knife or a pizza wheel, cut the dough circle into 8 equal triangles.

10. Roll up each triangle, starting with the wide end and ending with the pointed end.

STEP 9

11. Place the rugelach pointed ends down on a parchment-lined baking sheet. (It's important to line the baking sheet or any oozing apricot filling will stick to the pan while baking.) Sprinkle a few teaspoons of coarse sugar on the tops of the rugelach. Repeat with the remaining dough portions and filling.

12. Bake for 12 minutes. Using oven mitts or pot holders, carefully open the oven and turn the pan 180 degrees. Continue baking for 13 to 16 more minutes, until golden brown.

STEP 10

13. Using oven mitts or pot holders, carefully remove the rugelach from the oven and cool completely on the baking sheet before serving.

ITALIAN CANNOLI
(kan-OH-lee)

The type of ricotta cheese that you use will make all the difference with this Italian favorite. Try asking for fresh ricotta at a specialty cheese shop or Italian market. For some extra fun, you can dip the ends of the stuffed cannoli in chopped nuts or candied fruits.

DID YOU KNOW . . .

Cannoli originated on the Italian island of Sicily and are sometimes called "Turkish hats." It is said they date back to the time when the Saracens inhabited the island in the first millennium, and some say even before then.

INGREDIENTS

15 ounces fresh ricotta cheese (about 1½ cups)

3 tablespoons sugar

¼ teaspoon vanilla extract

¼ cup semisweet chocolate morsels, chopped

6 large prepared cannoli shells

TOOLS

Measuring cups and spoons • cutting board • chef's knife •

medium colander or strainer • large mixing bowl • cheesecloth • plastic wrap • medium mixing bowl • spoon or rubber spatula • scissors (optional) • pastry bag or plastic resealable food storage bag • large piping tip (optional)

DIRECTIONS   CAUTION

1. Place a medium colander or strainer inside a large mixing bowl, making sure that the bottom of the colander does not touch the bottom of the bowl. Line the inside of the colander with 1 piece of cheesecloth, folded in half.

2. Place the ricotta cheese inside the cheesecloth and cover with plastic wrap. Refrigerate for 24 hours to let the excess liquid drain off the ricotta.

3. Remove from the refrigerator. Raise the cheesecloth and ricotta above the bowl and gently squeeze the cheesecloth to remove any excess liquid.

4. Place the ricotta in a medium mixing bowl and stir in the sugar. Add the vanilla and chopped chocolate, stirring to combine with a spoon or rubber spatula.

5. Fit a pastry bag with a large piping tip, or cut off the bottom corner of a plastic food storage bag and stick the piping tip through the opening (page 23). The filling can also be piped from the bag without a piping tip if you cut a smaller hole. It is best to work quickly with this filling, so that the mixture doesn't get too soft.

STEP 5

6. Using a spoon or rubber spatula, place the ricotta filling inside the bag. Squeeze the filling down toward the tip.

7. Gently squeeze the filling into each end of the cannoli shells.

Note: Serve the cannoli before the shells get soggy. They're fine after a few hours in the refrigerator, but it's best to fill them just before serving.

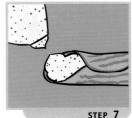

STEP 7

OLD-FASHIONED APPLE PIE

This is an American classic! I like to serve this pie with a big scoop of vanilla ice cream while the pie is still slightly warm.

Some people prefer to heat a piece of Cheddar cheese on the top of their pie. However you choose to eat it, it is guaranteed to please! Bring one to your next family get-together!

DID YOU KNOW . . .

While apples have been around since before the Stone Age, they are not native to the Americas. The Spaniard explorers brought apples to Mexico and South America and the Pilgrims planted apple seeds in 1692.

INGREDIENTS

1 recipe Basic Sweet Pie Dough
(recipe on page 189)

2¾ pounds Golden Delicious
apples, peeled, cored, and
sliced about ¼ inch thick (5 to
6 apples, about 7 cups sliced)
(page 15)

1 tablespoon fresh lemon juice

¾ cup light brown sugar

3 tablespoons all-purpose flour

¾ teaspoon ground cinnamon

⅛ teaspoon freshly grated nutmeg

Pinch of salt

1 large egg, lightly beaten

1 tablespoon water

1 teaspoon granulated sugar

TOOLS

Measuring cups and spoons •
cutting board • chef's knife •
paring knife • juicer (optional) •
grater (optional) • rolling pin •
9-inch pie pan • plastic wrap •
baking sheet • large mixing bowl •
fork or spoon • small mixing bowl
• wooden spoon • kitchen scissors
• paring knife • whisk • pastry
brush • oven mitts or pot holders •
aluminum foil

DIRECTIONS

CAUTION

1. Position rack in bottom third of oven and preheat the oven to 425°F.

2. Prepare the pie dough per instructions on page 189. On a lightly floured
surface, use a rolling pin to roll out the larger half of the pie dough into
a 13-inch circle. Place the circle of dough inside a 9-inch pie pan so that
it hangs over the edges of the pie pan. Cover loosely with plastic wrap
and refrigerate for 20 minutes.

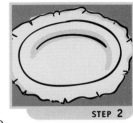
STEP 2

3. Roll out the remaining half of the pie dough on a lightly floured surface to
about 14 inches in diameter. Gently place the dough circle on a lightly floured
baking sheet, cover loosely with plastic wrap, and refrigerate for 20 minutes.

4. Place the sliced apples, lemon juice, and sugar in a large mixing bowl and
toss with a fork or spoon to combine.

5. In a small mixing bowl, stir together the flour, cinnamon, nutmeg, and salt,
then sprinkle over the apples.

6. Toss the flour mixture with the apples and allow the mixture to sit for 10
minutes.

7. Remove the piecrusts from the refrigerator. Fill the bottom crust with the
apple mixture, mounding the apples into the pie plate.

STEP 8

8. Top the pie with the remaining dough circle, allowing the edges to hang
over the sides of the dish. Using kitchen
scissors, trim the dough so that only an inch
hangs over the edges, pinching the top and
bottom crusts together as you trim. Fold the
extra inch of dough under and tuck it into
the pie pan, pressing gently so that the
dough does not unfold while baking. Using
your index fingers and thumbs, go around
the edges of the pie crimping the dough in a
wavy pattern (page 26).

(continued)

9. Using a paring knife, cut several small slits in the top of the pie to allow steam to escape while baking.

10. Whisk together the egg and water. Using a pastry brush, lightly brush the mixture onto the top of the pie. Sprinkle the top with the granulated sugar. Refrigerate the pie for 15 minutes.

11. Place the pie on a baking sheet and bake for 20 minutes.

12. After 20 minutes, reduce the oven temperature to 350°F and bake for an additional 25 minutes.

13. With oven mitts or pot holders, remove the baking sheet from the oven and cover the pie lightly with aluminum foil to make sure it doesn't get too brown. Return the sheet to the oven and bake an additional 20 to 25 minutes. Remove the aluminum foil for the last 5 minutes of baking for a nice brown crust, if desired. Just be careful to use oven mitts or pot holders.

14. Using oven mitts or pot holders, remove the pie from the oven and allow to rest until cooled, about 1 hour.

BASIC SWEET PIE DOUGH

YIELD: Two (9- or 10-inch) single piecrusts or 1 double-crust pie

INGREDIENTS

3¼ cups all-purpose flour

2 tablespoons sugar

1 teaspoon salt

1 cup (2 sticks) cold unsalted butter, cut into ½-inch pieces

¼ cup cold solid vegetable shortening

5 to 6 tablespoons ice water

TOOLS

Measuring cups and spoons • paring knife • sifter • large mixing bowl • pastry cutter (optional) • plastic wrap

DIRECTIONS   CAUTION

1. Sift the flour, sugar, and salt into a large mixing bowl.

2. Using your fingertips or a pastry cutter, work the butter and shortening into the flour until the mixture resembles small peas.

3. Work the ice water into the mixture with your fingers just until the dough comes together; be careful not to overmix.

4. Form the dough into two disks, making one slightly larger than the other, and wrap each disk individually in plastic wrap.

5. Refrigerate for at least 30 minutes or overnight before rolling out.

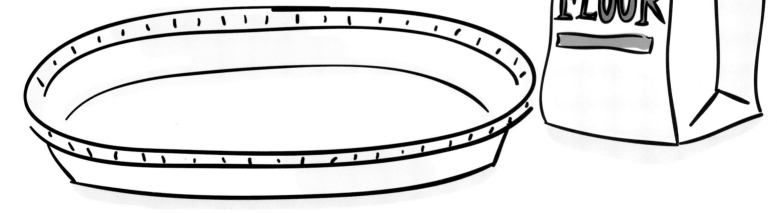

CHOCOLATE COOKIE-PEANUT BUTTER BANANA PIE

Everyone loves Oreos! So we've made a crispy crunchy Oreo piecrust for this frozen peanut butter pie, and added some bananas to—you know—kick it up a notch or two! Don't miss this most American of dessert treats.

DIRECTIONS   CAUTION 👁 🔪 🔥 🧤 🔌

1. In the bowl of a food processor or blender, combine 16 of the chocolate sandwich cookies and ¼ cup of the peanuts. Process until finely crumbled.

2. Place the crumbs in a medium mixing bowl and drizzle with the melted butter, stirring until moistened. Press the crumb mixture into a 9-inch pie pan, covering the bottom and sides evenly. Chill the piecrust in the refrigerator for 20 minutes.

   CAUTION Be careful to keep your fingers and utensils away from rotating beaters when adding ingredients to a running mixer.

190

INGREDIENTS

16 cream-filled chocolate sandwich cookies, plus 4 for garnish (optional)

1/4 cup plus 2 tablespoons honey-roasted peanuts

2 tablespoons unsalted butter, melted

1 cup creamy peanut butter

1 (8-ounce) package cream cheese, softened

1 1/2 cups confectioners' sugar

1 cup heavy cream

2 small bananas

TOOLS

Measuring cups and spoons • small saucepan • paring knife • food processor or blender • medium mixing bowl • 9-inch pie pan • standing electric mixer with paddle and whisk attachments • large mixing bowl • rubber spatula • wooden spoon • plastic wrap • oven mitts or pot holders

DID YOU KNOW. . .

Africans ground peanuts into stews as early as the fifteenth century, and the ancient Chinese used them in cooking as well. The Spanish explorers were the first to trade peanuts to the American colonies.

3. In the bowl of a standing electric mixer fitted with a paddle attachment, combine the peanut butter and cream cheese. Mix on low until creamy. With the mixer still on low, gradually add the confectioners' sugar, mixing until combined. Turn the mixer off, remove the peanut butter mixture, and place in a large mixing bowl.

4. Clean the bowl of the mixer and remove the paddle attachment. Add the whisk attachment and, in the clean bowl, whisk the cream on medium-high until stiff peaks form. Turn the mixer off.

STEP 5

5. Using a rubber spatula, gently fold the whipped cream into the peanut butter mixture, adding the cream a little at a time, and being careful not to overmix.

6. Peel and slice the bananas, about 1/4 inch thick. Lay the banana slices in one even layer in the bottom of the chilled piecrust.

STEP 6

7. Spoon the peanut butter filling into the piecrust over the bananas and smooth the top with the back of the spoon. (The filling will be taller than the edges of the piecrust.)

8. Cover the pie lightly with plastic wrap and freeze for 4 hours or overnight.

STEP 7

9. To serve, cut the 4 remaining sandwich cookies in half and place the cookie halves around the top of the pie. Chop the remaining 2 tablespoons of peanuts and sprinkle over the top of the pie. Cut into 8 even slices.

Note: If the pie has been frozen for longer than 4 hours, allow it to sit for 10 to 15 minutes before slicing.

CARIBBEAN BAKED BANANAS

This popular dish is enjoyed on many Caribbean islands. You just can't go wrong with bananas, brown sugar, butter, and spices. We make a version of this in New Orleans, except ours is cooked in a sauté pan with the addition of rum—we call it Bananas Foster. I think you'll love this dessert. It's not only delicious but also super easy to prepare. Don't forget the ice cream for a showstopping finish!

INGREDIENTS

3 bananas, peeled and sliced in half lengthwise and crosswise

1 tablespoon unsalted butter

½ cup light brown sugar

½ teaspoon ground cinnamon

¼ teaspoon freshly ground nutmeg

½ cup fresh orange juice

Vanilla ice cream

TOOLS

Measuring cups and spoons • cutting board • chef's knife or paring knife • 11 x 7-inch baking dish • small saucepan • wooden spoon • tongs • oven mitts or pot holders

DIRECTIONS   CAUTION

1. Position rack in center of oven and preheat the oven to 350°F.

2. Place the bananas flat, cut side down, in the bottom of an 11 by 7-inch baking dish. Set aside.

3. In a small saucepan over medium-high heat, combine the butter, brown sugar, cinnamon, and nutmeg, stirring until the sugar begins to melt. Add the orange juice and bring the mixture to a boil. Boil for 1 minute, until slightly thickened.

4. Using oven mitts or pot holders, carefully pour the warm sauce over the bananas. Transfer to the oven and bake for 10 minutes.

STEP 4

5. Using oven mitts or pot holders, remove the baking dish from the oven and, using tongs, carefully turn the bananas over so that the cut side is facing up. Carefully return the dish to the oven and bake for an additional 10 minutes.

STEP 5

6. Allow the bananas to cool slightly before serving. Serve the warm sauce and bananas over vanilla ice cream.

CHOCOLATE-HAZELNUT BISCOTTI

(bee-SKAWT-tee)

Biscotti means "twice cooked" in Italian, referring to the two times that these crisp cookies are baked in the oven. They are often dipped in coffee to soften them as a coffee-time treat. Try serving them with hot chocolate instead, for a doubly chocolaty dessert.

DID YOU KNOW . . .

Biscotti have always been ideal food for sailors because they keep so well. In fact, Christopher Columbus had them on his voyage in 1492.

INGREDIENTS

1¹⁄₃ cups all-purpose flour

¹⁄₂ cup Dutch-processed cocoa
   powder

1 cup sugar

³⁄₄ teaspoon baking soda

¹⁄₈ teaspoon salt

³⁄₄ cup toasted hazelnuts, roughly
   chopped

¹⁄₃ cup semisweet chocolate
   morsels

2 large eggs plus 1 egg yolk

³⁄₄ teaspoon vanilla extract

TOOLS

Measuring cups and spoons •
cutting board • chef's knife •
baking sheet • parchment paper •
standing electric mixer fitted with
paddle attachment • small mixing
bowl • whisk • rubber spatula •
oven mitts or pot holders •
serrated knife • wire rack • metal
spatula • airtight container

DIRECTIONS

CAUTION

1. Position rack in center of oven and preheat the oven to 325°F. Line a baking sheet with parchment paper and set aside.

> CAUTION
> Be careful to keep your fingers and utensils away from rotating beaters when adding ingredients to a running mixer.

2. In the bowl of a standing electric mixer fitted with a paddle attachment, combine the flour, cocoa powder, sugar, baking soda, and salt. Mix on low to combine. Turn the mixer off and add the hazelnuts and chocolate morsels and mix on low.

3. In a small mixing bowl, whisk together the eggs, egg yolk, and vanilla. With the mixer still on low, add the egg mixture to the flour mixture, combining just until the dough comes together. Turn the mixer off.

4. Using a rubber spatula, scrape the dough out onto a well-floured surface and knead lightly to work in any extra flour mixture from the bottom of the mixing bowl.

5. Form the dough into a long log, about 3¹⁄₃ inches wide. Using your hands, flatten the top of the dough.

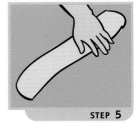

STEP 5

6. Place the dough log onto the prepared baking sheet and bake for 45 to 50 minutes. The log should become firm, with cracks in the top, and the dough should be completely dry to the touch.

7. Using oven mitts or pot holders, remove the log from the oven and cool slightly on the baking sheet.

8. Reduce the oven temperature to 300°F.

9. When the log is cool enough to handle, remove it from the baking sheet and cut into 12 slices, about ¹⁄₂ inch thick, on a slight diagonal.

STEP 9

10. Lay the slices flat on the parchment-lined baking sheet and bake for an additional 30 to 35 minutes.

11. Using oven mitts or pot holders, remove the biscotti from the oven. Using a metal spatula, carefully move the biscotti to a wire rack and cool completely.

12. Store in an airtight container.

FRUIT GALETTE
(gah-LEHT)

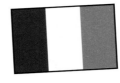

In France, a galette can be any of a number of flat, disk-shaped cakes, pies, or tarts, either savory or sweet. My version here is a great fruit tart for beginning cooks: You make a simple piecrust and roll it out, then fill it with fresh, ripe fruit, and bake the tart without a pie pan for a rustic, country feel. If your pastry happens to break or tear while you're working with it, don't worry—simply moisten the tear with a bit of water and pinch it back together. Hey, it's not rocket science!

INGREDIENTS

Crust:

1½ cups plus 2 tablespoons all purpose flour

3 tablespoons sugar

½ teaspoon salt

8 tablespoons cold unsalted butter, cut into ½-inch pieces

2 tablespoons cold vegetable shortening

3 tablespoons ice water

Fruit filling:

3 cups thinly sliced peaches

1 cup mixed berries, such as blackberries and cherries, rinsed well and picked over

½ cup plus 1 tablespoon sugar

2 tablespoons cornstarch

1 teaspoon fresh lemon juice

TOOLS

Measuring cups and spoons • paring knife • large mixing bowl • pastry cutter or two knives (optional) • plastic wrap • rolling pin • parchment paper • rimmed baking sheet • large mixing bowl • juicer (optional) • pastry brush • 2 metal spatulas (optional) • oven mitts or pot holders • wire rack

DIRECTIONS   CAUTION

1. Combine the flour, sugar, and salt in a large mixing bowl. Add the butter and shortening and, using a pastry cutter, two knives, or your fingers, work the butter and shortening into the flour until the mixture resembles coarse crumbs.

STEP 1

2. Add the water, 1 tablespoon at a time, working it just until the pastry comes together. Form the dough into a disk and wrap in plastic wrap. Refrigerate for at least 1 hour and up to overnight.

3. When you are ready to bake the galette, position rack in center of oven and preheat the oven to 425°F. Remove the pie dough from the refrigerator and allow to warm up slightly.

4. On a lightly floured work surface, use a lightly floured rolling pin to roll the pastry to a thickness of about ⅛ inch. Sprinkle a bit more flour if necessary so that the pastry does not stick to the rolling pin or the work surface.

5. Carefully roll the pastry onto the rolling pin and transfer to a parchment-lined rimmed baking sheet. Refrigerate while you prepare the fruit.

6. Combine the peaches, berries, ½ cup of the sugar, cornstarch, and lemon juice in a large mixing bowl and toss gently to combine.

7. Remove the pastry from the refrigerator and place the fruit in the center of the crust, leaving a 4-inch border. Gently fold the edges of the crust up and over the fruit so that the pastry forms a sort of bowl. Brush the top edges of the crust with a little water and sprinkle with the remaining tablespoon of sugar.

STEP 7

8. Bake for 20 minutes, until the crust is set and lightly golden around the edges. Reduce the heat to 375°F and continue to bake until the crust is golden brown and the fruit is bubbly inside, about 20 minutes longer.

9. Using oven mitts or pot holders, transfer the baking sheet to a wire rack and allow to cool slightly before carefully transferring the galette to a serving plate. (Two metal spatulas work well for this.) Serve warm with vanilla ice cream, crème fraiche, or sweetened whipped cream, if desired.

WEBSITE GUIDE

Chef Emeril Lagasse
www.emerils.com

The official website for everything Emeril. Here you will find listings for all his restaurants, shows, merchandise, and in-depth background and insight into Emeril's culinary world, as well as weekly menus with recipes, kitchen tips, fun food talk, and lots of great information. . . . Bam!

The Emeril Lagasse Foundation
www.emeril.org

The foundation seeks to inspire and enable young people to realize their full potential by supporting programs that create developmental and educational opportunities within the communities where Emeril's restaurants operate.

All-Clad Cookware
www.emerilware.com

The cookware that Chef Emeril believes in. Here you will find the entire range of Emerilware by All-Clad, from skillets to sauté pans.

B&G Foods
www.bgfoods.com

If you want to kick up your kitchen a notch, look for Emeril's original spice blends, salad dressings, marinades, hot sauces, and pasta sauces distributed by B&G Foods and available at supermarkets nationwide.

Food Network
www.foodtv.com

Log on to the Food Network's site for all recipes and scheduling information for *Emeril Live* and *The Essence of Emeril* shows, and ticket information for *Emeril Live*.

Good Morning America
http://abcnews.go.com

Wake up to Chef Emeril on Friday mornings on ABC, when he shares his culinary creations with America.

HarperCollins Publishers
www.harpercollins.com

This informative site offers background on and chapter excerpts from all of Chef Emeril's best-selling cookbooks.

New Orleans Fish House
www.nofishhouse.com

Emeril's Gulf Shrimp are certified Wild American Shrimp packaged and distributed by New Orleans Fish House.

Pride of San Juan
www.prideofsanjuan.com

Emeril Lagasse and Pride of San Juan have partnered to bring you fresh, high-quality produce. Emeril's Gourmet Produce brand launches with an innovative selection of pre-packaged salads and herb packs.

Sanita Clogs
www.sanitaclogs.com

Emeril and Sanita Clogs have teamed up to provide you with a new clog especially made for Emeril and You! Sanita Clogs have produced quality Danish clogs since 1907.

Sara Lee Foods
www.emerilsgourmetmeats.com

Emeril's Gourmet Meats offer bold, full-flavored meat products with consistent top quality. It will take your dinner to a whole new level.

Waterford/Wedgwood
www.wwusa.com

The world's leading luxury lifestyle group produces Emeril At Home, a classic addition to the home kitchen.

Wüsthof Knives
www.wusthof.com

Emerilware Knives gift and block sets, made to Emeril's specifications by one of the world's foremost manufacturers of quality cutlery.

EMERIL'S
RESTAURANT GUIDE

Emeril's Restaurant

800 Tchoupitoulas Street
New Orleans, LA 70130
(504) 528–9393

NOLA

534 St. Louis Street
New Orleans, LA 70130
(504) 522–6652

Emeril's Delmonico

1300 St. Charles Avenue
New Orleans, LA 70130
(504) 525–4937

Emeril's New Orleans Fish House
AT THE MGM GRAND HOTEL AND CASINO

3799 Las Vegas Boulevard South
Las Vegas, NV 89109
(702) 891–7374

Delmonico Steakhouse
AT THE VENETIAN RESORT AND CASINO

3355 Las Vegas Boulevard South
Las Vegas, NV 89109
(702) 414–3737

Emeril's Orlando

6000 Universal Boulevard
at Universal Studios CityWalk
Orlando, FL 32819
(407) 224–2424

Emeril's Tchoup Chop
AT UNIVERSAL ORLANDO'S ROYAL PACIFIC RESORT

6300 Hollywood Way
Orlando, FL 32819
(407) 503-2467

Emeril's Atlanta
ONE ALLIANCE CENTER

3500 Lenox Road
Atlanta, GA 30326
(404) 564-5600

Emeril's Miami Beach
AT LOEWS MIAMI BEACH HOTEL

1601 Collins Avenue
Miami Beach, FL 33139
(305) 695-4550